Pakistan Travel Guide.

Tourism

Author
Jesse Russell.

Publisher:
SONITTEC LTD
College House, 2nd
Floor
17 King Edwards
Road,
Ruislip
London
HA4 7AE

Table of Content

Summary

How Traveling Can Broaden Your Perspective

<u>Pakistan Guide</u>: You may not need a lot of convincing when it comes to finding a reason to travel especially when considering a trip to a foreign country. Exploring the world, seeing new places, and learning about new cultures are just a few of the benefits of traveling. There is value to exploring someplace new and combating the stress of getting out of your comfort zone.

Traveling should be looked at as a journey for personal growth, mental health, and spiritual enlightenment. Taking the time to travel to a new place can both literally and figuratively open your eyes to things you have never seen before. These new experiences allow you to get to know yourself in ways you can't if you stay in the same place.

✓ Traveling is wonderful in so many ways:

✓ You can indulge your sense of wanderlust.

✓ You experience different cultures.

✓ Your taste buds get to experience unique foods.

✓ You meet all different kinds of people.

As you grow older, your mind evolves and expands to adapt to the new information you receive. Traveling to a new destination is similar in this way, but the learning process occurs at a faster rate. Traveling thrusts you into the unknown and delivers you with a bounty of new information and ideas. The expansion of your mind is one of the greatest benefits of travel. Keep reading to learn six more benefits of traveling.

> Discover Your Purpose: Feeling as though you have a purpose in life is more important than many people realize. A purpose connects you to something bigger than yourself and keeps you moving forward. Your purpose in life can change suddenly and fluidly as you enter new stages in becoming who you are. With each new stage in life, there comes new goals and callings. Traveling can help open your eyes to a new life direction. You may be wandering down a path unaware of where you will end up. Seeing new places and meeting new people can help you break from that path and discover what your true purpose is.

Traveling is an excellent remedy for when you feel you need to refocus on your purpose and goals, or re-evaluate your life path. There is no better time to open your eyes than when your life seems to be out of focus and in need of redirection. You might just be surprised by what you discover and find a new sense of life purpose how traveling changes you.

Traveling is a way to discover parts of yourself that you never knew existed. While traveling, you have no choice but to deal with unexpected situations. For example, how you may typically handle a problem at home might be a completely unacceptable approach when you are in an unfamiliar place without all of the comforts and conveniences of home.

> Be Aware of Your Blessings: When you travel to a new destination, your eyes are opened to new standards, and, you become more aware of all the blessings and privileges you have been given. It is easy to forget what you do have and only focus on what is missing from your life. Traveling can help put things back into perspective and re-center your priorities on what truly matters.

Consider traveling through an area that has no electricity or running water if you come from a place where cold bottled water is easily accessible and nearly anything you want can be delivered to your door in less than an hour. These are two completely different worlds and ways of living. For people who experience a more privileged quality of life, seeing others who live in drastically different situations can help you appreciate what you have and spark an interest for you to lend support to people living elsewhere.

> Find Truth: There's concept, and then there's experience. You can know things from reading them online and listening to a lecture, but to experience something in person is different.

Traveling can help open your eyes to the true kindness and goodness of humanity. There is a myth that when you travel you are on your own, but that simply is not the case. The welcoming attitude and overwhelming hospitality that people give to travelers may be one of the most surprising truths about traveling. Beyond that, you have the whole world to learn about with every place you discover, through every person you meet and every culture you experience.

> Expand Your Mind: A key benefit of traveling, or taking the opportunity to explore on a vacation, is being given the opportunity to expand your mind in ways you can't imagine. If you can allow yourself to travel with an open mind and accept the new experiences and adventures around you, you give your mind the chance to see the world from a new perspective.

Think of it as a spiritual and intellectual enlightenment. You never stop being curious and should always seek out education whenever possible throughout your life. You are doing a disservice to yourself if you choose to close yourself off from the world. It is not always easy to let new ideas in, especially when they are in direct contrast with what you may believe. You have everything you need to grow, you just have to allow yourself to do it.

> Connect to Others: It's easy to forget how similar you are to others, regardless of where you come from, what your background is, or how much money you have. At the end of the day, human beings share more in common with one another than they may choose to admit. When taking a trip to a different country, you may have learned to cast aside what is different and unusual because from the outside, others may not look or act alike. But if you give yourself a chance, you may be surprised to find how minimal and superficial these differences are.

As you notice how you share similar needs, your perspective of your home expands, you become friends with people from different backgrounds and cultures, you realize how everyone is connected. This state of awareness is a jump in consciousness that can help you experience a world-centric view of consciousness more expansive and aware.

> Break Out of Your Shell: Without a doubt, one of the benefits of traveling is that it forces you to step out of your bubble, which can provide you with many emotional health benefits. Yes, it may be uncomfortable and scary to break away from your daily routine, but the rewards are worth it. What you gain in experience and knowledge may outweigh any amount of doubt or apprehension you had before embarking on your journey. Travel also helps you to self-reflect and dig deep into who you are as a person.

Something magical happens when people are put in new situations than they are normally faced with in their everyday life, as behavior becomes more raw and real as a result of being out of your conditioned environment. This not-so-subtle push into the world helps you to become more open and comfortable expressing yourself without the worry of feeling judged.

> See the Big Picture: Life is a limited gift. You must choose to make the most of each day. As you travel and experience more of the world, you may be struck with gratitude and appreciation for all the places you have enjoyed and people you've shared your travels with. You have the power to take control of your life and can inspire you to start doing more.

Introduction

Pakistan, populous and multiethnic country of South Asia. Having a predominately Indo-Iranian speaking population, Pakistan has historically and culturally been associated with its neighbours Iran, Afghanistan, and India. Since Pakistan and India achieved independence in 1947, Pakistan has been distinguished from its larger southeastern neighbour by its overwhelmingly Muslim population (as opposed to the predominance of Hindus in India). Pakistan has struggled throughout its existence to attain political stability and sustained social development. Its capital is Islamabad, in the foothills of the Himalayas in the northern part of the country, and its largest city is Karachi, in the south on the coast of the Arabian Sea.

Pakistan was brought into being at the time of the partition of British India, in response to the demands of Islamic nationalists: as articulated by the All India Muslim League under the leadership of Mohammed Ali Jinnah, India's Muslims would receive just representation only in their own country. From independence until 1971, Pakistan (both de facto and in law) consisted of two regions West Pakistan, in the Indus River basin in the northwestern portion of the Indian subcontinent, and East Pakistan, located more than 1,000 miles (1,600 km) to the east in the vast delta of the Ganges-Brahmaputra river system. In response to grave internal political problems that erupted in civil war in 1971, East Pakistan was proclaimed the independent country of Bangladesh.

Pakistan encompasses a rich diversity of landscapes, starting in the northwest, from the soaring Pamirs and the Karakoram Range through a maze of mountain ranges, a complex of valleys, and inhospitable plateaus, down to the remarkably even surface of the fertile Indus River plain, which drains southward into the Arabian Sea. It contains a section of the ancient Silk Road and the Khyber Pass, the famous passageway that has brought outside influences into the otherwise isolated subcontinent. Lofty peaks such as K2 and Nanga Parbat, in the Pakistani-administered region of Kashmir, present a challenging lure to mountain climbers. Along the Indus River, the artery of the country, the ancient site of Mohenjo-daro marks one of the cradles of civilization.

Yet, politically and culturally, Pakistan has struggled to define itself. Established as a parliamentary democracy that espoused secular ideas, the country has experienced repeated military coups, and religion that is to say, adherence to the values of Sunni Islam has increasingly become a standard by which political leaders are measured. In addition, northern Pakistan particularly the Federally Administered

Tribal Areas has become a haven for members of neighbouring Afghanistan's ousted Taliban regime and for members of numerous other Islamic extremist groups. In various parts of the country, instances of ethnic, religious, and social conflict have flared up from time to time, often rendering those areas virtually ungovernable by the central authorities, and acts of violence against religious minorities have increased.

At the time of partition in 1947, as many as 10 million Muslim refugees fled their homes in India and sought refuge in Pakistan about 8 million in West Pakistan. Virtually an equal number of Hindus and Sikhs were uprooted from their land and familiar surroundings in what became Pakistan, and they fled to India. Unlike the earlier migrations, which took centuries to unfold, these chaotic population transfers took hardly one year. The resulting impact on the life of the subcontinent has reverberated ever since in the rivalries between the two countries, and each has continued to seek a lasting modus vivendi with the other. Pakistan and India have fought four wars, three of which (1948–49, 1965, and 1999) were over Kashmir. Since 1998 both countries have also possessed nuclear weapons, further heightening tensions between them.

About Pakistan

The Land

Pakistan is bounded by Iran to the west, Afghanistan to the northwest and north, China to the northeast, and India to the east and southeast. The coast of the Arabian Sea forms its southern border.

Since 1947 the Kashmir region, along the western Himalayas, has been disputed, with Pakistan, India, and China each controlling sections of the territory. Part of the Pakistani-administered territory comprises the so-called Azad Kashmir ("Free Kashmir") region which Pakistan nonetheless considers an independent state, with its capital at Muzaffarabad. The remainder of Pakistani-administered Kashmir consists of Gilgit and Baltistan, known collectively as the Northern Areas.

Relief and drainage

Pakistan is situated at the western end of the great Indo-Gangetic Plain. Of the total area of the country, about three-fifths consists of rough mountainous terrain and plateaus, and the remaining two-fifths constitutes a wide expanse of level plain. The land can be divided into five major regions: the Himalayan and Karakoram ranges and their subranges; the Hindu Kush and western mountains; the Balochistan plateau; the submontane plateau (Potwar Plateau, Salt Range, trans-Indus plain, and Sialkot area); and the Indus River plain. Within each major division there are further subdivisions, including a number of desert areas.

The Himalayan and Karakoram ranges

The Himalayas, which have long been a physical and cultural divide between South and Central Asia, form the northern rampart of the subcontinent, and their western ranges occupy the entire northern end of Pakistan, extending about 200 miles (320 km) into the country. Spreading over Kashmir and northern Pakistan, the western Himalayan system splits into three distinct ranges, which are, from south to north, the Pir Panjal Range, the Zaskar Range, and the Ladakh Range. Farther north is the Karakoram Range, which is a separate system adjoining the Himalayas. This series of ranges varies in elevation from roughly 13,000 feet (4,000 metres) to higher than 19,500 feet (6,000 metres) above sea level. Four of the region's peaks exceed 26,000 feet (8,000 metres), and many rise to heights of more than 15,000 feet (4,500 metres). These include such towering peaks as Nanga Parbat (26,660 feet [8,126 metres]) and K2, also called Godwin Austen (28,251 feet [8,611 metres]), in the Northern Areas.

Several important rivers flow from, or through, the mountains of Kashmir into Pakistan. From the Pir Panjal Range flows the Jhelum River (which bisects the famous Vale of Kashmir); the Indus River descends between the Zaskar and Ladakh ranges; and the Shyok River rises in the Karakoram Range. South of the Pir Panjal is the northwestern extension of the Shiwalik Range (there rising to about 600 to 900 feet [200 to 300 metres]), which extend over the southern part of the Hazara and Murree hills and include the hills surrounding Rawalpindi and neighbouring Islamabad.

Beyond the Karakoram Range in the extreme north lies the Uygur Autonomous Region of Xinjiang, China; to the northwest, beyond the Hindu Kush, are the Pamirs, where only the Vākhān (Wakhan Corridor), a narrow strip of Afghan territory, separates Pakistan from Tajikistan. The Himalayan massif was pierced in 1970 when Chinese and Pakistani engineers completed the Karakoram Highway across the Karakoram Range, linking the town of Gilgit in the Northern Areas with Kashgar (Kashi) in Xinjiang. The highway, a marvel of modern technology, carries considerable commerce between the two countries but has promoted little cultural exchange.

The northern mountain barrier influences the precipitation pattern in Pakistan by intercepting monsoon (rain-bearing) winds from the south. Melting snow and glacial meltwater from the mountains also feed the rivers, including the Indus, which emerge from the east-west-aligned ranges to flow southward. Siachen Glacier, one of the world's longest mountain glaciers, feeds the Nubra River, a tributary of the Shyok. The many glaciers in this region, particularly those of the Karakoram Range, are among the few in the world to have grown in size since the late 20th century.

The northern and western regions of the country are subject to frequent seismic activity the natural consequence of a geologically young mountain system. Minor earth tremors are common throughout the region. However, a number of earthquakes have been severe and highly destructive, given the fact that many buildings are poorly constructed and that those in the mountains are often precipitously perched. Historically recent major quakes in Pakistan include those in 1935, 1945, 1974, and 2005. The latter two were in the far north of the country, and the 2005 quake centred in the mountainous border region of the North-West Frontier Province (now Khyber Pakhtunkhwa) and Azad Kashmir killed some 80,000 to 90,000 people and left the entire area devastated.

The population in this inhospitable northern region is generally sparse, although in a few favoured places it is dense. In most of the tiny settlements of this region, the usual crop is barley; fruit cultivation, especially apricots, is of special importance. Timber, mainly species of pine, is found in some parts, but its occurrence varies with precipitation and elevation. Many slopes have been denuded of cover by excessive timber felling and overgrazing.

The Hindu Kush and the western mountains

In far northern Pakistan the Hindu Kush branches off southwestward from the nodal orogenic uplift known as the Pamir Knot. The ridges of the Hindu Kush generally trend from northeast to southwest, while those of the Karakorams run in a southeast-northwest direction from the knot. The Hindu Kush is made up of two distinct ranges, a main crest line that is cut by transverse streams, and a watershed range to the west of the main range, in Afghanistan, that divides the Indus system of rivers from the Amu Darya (ancient Oxus River) drainage basin. From the Hindu Kush, several branches run southward through the areas of Chitral, Dir, and Swat, in Khyber Pakhtunkhwa. These branches have deep, narrow valleys along the Kunar, Panjkora, and Swat rivers. In the extreme northern portion, the ranges are capped with perpetual snow and ice; high peaks include Tirich Mir, which rises to 25,230 feet (7,690 metres). The valley sides are generally bare on account of their isolation from the precipitation-bearing influences. Toward the south the region is largely covered with forests of deodar (a type of cedar) and pine and also has extensive grasslands.

The Safid Mountain Range, lying south of the Kābul River and forming a border with Afghanistan, trends roughly east to west and rises throughout to an elevation of about 14,000 feet (4,300 metres). Its outliers are spread over Kohat district, Khyber Pakhtunkhwa. South of the Safid Range are the hills of Waziristan, which are crossed by the Kurram and Tochi rivers, and even farther south is the Gumal River. Comparatively broad mountain passes are located south of the Kābul River. They are, from north to south, the Khyber, Kurram, Tochi, Gomal, and Bolan. The Khyber Pass is of special historical interest: broad enough to allow for the passing of large numbers of troops, it has often been the point of ingress for armies invading the subcontinent.

South of the Gumal River, the Sulaiman Range runs in a roughly north-south direction. The highest point of that range, Takht-e Sulaiman, has twin peaks, the higher of which reaches 18,481 feet (5,633 metres). The Sulaiman Range tapers into the Marri and Bugti hills in the south. The Sulaiman and, farther south, the low Kirthar Range separate the Balochistan plateau from the Indus plain.

The Balochistan plateau

The vast tableland of Balochistan contains a great variety of physical features. In the northeast a basin centred on the towns of Zhob and Loralai forms a trellis-patterned lobe that is surrounded on all sides by mountain ranges. To the east and southeast is the Sulaiman Range, which joins the Central Brahui Range near Quetta, and to the north and northwest is the Toba Kakar Range (which farther west becomes the Khwaja Amran Range). The hilly terrain becomes less severe southwestward in the form of Ras Koh Range. The small Quetta basin is surrounded on all sides by mountains. The whole area appears to form a node of high ranges. West of the Ras Koh Range, the general landform of northwestern Balochistan is a series of low-lying plateaus divided by hills. In the north the Chagai Hills border a region of true desert, consisting of inland drainage and hamuns (playas).

Southern Balochistan is a vast wilderness of mountain ranges, of which the Central Brahui Range is the backbone. The easternmost Kirthar Range is backed by the Pab Range in the west. Other important ranges of southern Balochistan are the Central Makran Range and the Makran Coast Range, whose steep face to the south divides the coastal plain from the rest of the plateau. The Makran coastal track mostly comprises level mud flats surrounded by sandstone ridges. The isolation of the arid plain has been broken by an ongoing development project at Gwadar, which is linked with Karachi via an improved road transport system.

The submontane plateau

Lying south of the northern mountain rampart, the submontane plateau has four distinct divisions the Trans-Indus plains, the Potwar Plateau, the Salt Range, and the Sialkot region.

The Trans-Indus plains, west of the Indus River, comprise the hill-girt plateaus of the Vale of Peshawar and of Kohat and Bannu, all of which are oases in the arid, scrub-covered landscape of Khyber

Pakhtunkhwa. Of these, the Vale of Peshawar is the most fertile. Gravel or clay alluvial detritus covers much of the area and is formed from loose particles or fragments separated from masses of rock by erosion and other forces. Annual precipitation is generally limited to between 10 and 15 inches (250 and 380 mm), and most of the cultivated area in the Vale of Peshawar is irrigated from canals.

Kohat is less developed than the Vale of Peshawar. Precipitation is about 16 inches (400 mm). Only a small percentage of the cultivated area is canal-irrigated, and its groundwater is not adequately exploited, although the water table is generally high. Much of the area consists of scrub and poor grazing land. The region is much broken by limestone ridges, and the uneven limestone floor is variously filled with lacustrine clays, gravel, or boulders.

In Bannu, about one-fourth of the cultivated area is irrigated. Annual precipitation is low, amounting to about 11 inches (275 mm). Fat-tailed sheep, camels, and donkeys are raised in Kohat and Bannu; wool is an important cash crop.

The Potwar Plateau covers an area of about 5,000 square miles (13,000 square km) and lies at an elevation of some 1,200 to 1,900 feet (350 to 575 metres). It is bounded on the east by the Jhelum River and on the west by the Indus River. On the north, the Kala Chitta Range and Margala Hills (at about 3,000 to 5,000 feet [900 to 1,500 metres]) form its boundary. Toward the south it gradually slopes into the Salt Range, which presents a steep face rising to about 2,000 feet (600 metres) even farther south. The middle of the Potwar Plateau is occupied by the structurally downwarped basin of the Soan River. The general terrain of the basin consists of interlaced ravines, which are locally known as khaderas and are set deep in the soft Shiwalik beds of which the whole area is composed. The surface layer of the area is formed of windblown loessic silt, deteriorating into sand and gravel toward the hill slopes. The small Rawalpindi plain in the north is the location of the twin cities of Rawalpindi and Islamabad.

The Potwar Plateau receives modest annual precipitation, averaging between 15 and 20 inches (380 to 510 mm). Though precipitation is somewhat higher in the northwest, the southwest is very arid. The landscape is dissected and eroded by streams that, during the rains, cut into the land and wash away the soil. The streams are generally deep set and are of little or no use for irrigation. It is generally a poor agricultural area, and its population puts excessive pressure on its resources.

The Salt Range is an extremely arid territory that marks the boundary between the submontane region and the Indus River plain to the south. The highest point of the Salt Range, Mount Sakesar, lies at 4,992 feet (1,522 metres). The Salt Range is of interest to geologists because it contains the most complete geologic sequence in the world, in which rocks from early Cambrian times (about 540 million years ago) to the Pleistocene Epoch (about 2,600,000 to 11,700 years ago) are exposed in an unbroken sequence.

The Sialkot region is a narrow submontane area in the northeast. Unlike the Potwar Plateau, it is a rich agricultural region. Precipitation varies from 25 to 35 inches (650 to 900 mm) per year, and the water table is high, facilitating well (and tube-well) irrigation; the soil is heavy and highly fertile. The population distribution is dense, and the land is divided into small farms on which intensive cultivation is practiced.

The Indus River plain

The Indus River plain is a vast expanse of fertile land, covering about 200,000 square miles (518,000 square km), with a gentle slope from the Himalayan piedmont in the north to the Arabian Sea in the south. The average gradient of the slope is no more than 1 foot per mile (1 metre per 5 km). Except for the micro relief, the plain is featureless. It is divisible into two sections, the upper and lower Indus plains, on account of their differing physiographic features. The upper Indus plain is drained by the Indus together with its tributaries, the Jhelum, Chenab, Ravi, Beas, and Sutlej rivers, forming a developed system of interfluves, known locally as doabs, in Punjab province (Persian panj āb, "five waters," in reference to the five rivers). In the lower plain the Indus River has a Nilotic character; i.e., it forms a single large river with no significant tributaries. The plain narrows to form a corridor near

Mithankot, where the Sulaiman Range comes close to the plain and the Indus merges with its last major tributary, the Panjnad River (which is itself merely the confluence of the five Punjab rivers). Flooding is a perennial problem, especially along the Indus, as a consequence of heavy rains (usually in July and August).

The upper Indus plain consists of three subdivisions: the Himalayan piedmont, the doabs, and the Sulaiman piedmont (referred to locally as the Derajat). The Himalayan piedmont, or the sub-Shiwalik zone, is a narrow strip of land where the rivers enter into the plain from their mountain stage, thereby giving each a somewhat steeper gradient. The zone is characterized by numerous rivulets, which have produced a broken topography in parts of the zone. These streams remain dry except in the rainy season, when they swell into gushing streams with considerable erosive power.

The doabs between the various rivers display similar micro relief, which comprises four distinct landforms active floodplains, meander floodplains, cover floodplains, and scalloped interfluves. An active floodplain (known locally as a khaddar or bet), which lies adjacent to a river, is often called "the summer bed of rivers," as it is inundated almost every rainy season. It is the scene of changing river channels, though protective bunds (levees) have been built at many places on the outer margin of the bet to contain the river water in the rainy season. Adjoining the active floodplain is the meander floodplain, which occupies higher ground away from the river and is littered with bars, oxbow lakes, extinct channels, and levees. The cover floodplain is an expanse of geologically recent alluvium, the result of sheet flooding, in which alluvium covers the former riverine features. The scalloped interfluves, or bars, are the central, higher parts of the doab, with old alluvium of relatively uniform texture. The boundaries of the scalloped features are formed by river-cut scarps at places over 20 feet (6 metres) high. The generally level surface of this section of the plain is broken into small pockets in Chiniot and at Sangla Hill, near the much denuded Kirana Hills, which stand out in jagged pinnacles. These hills are considered to be the outliers of the Aravali Range of India.

The largest but poorest of the doabs is the Sind (Sindh) Sagar Doab, which is mostly desert and is situated between the Indus and Jhelum rivers. The doabs that lie to the east of it, however, constitute the richest agricultural lands in the country. Until the advent of irrigation, at the end of the 19th century, much of the area was a desolate waste, because of the low amount of precipitation. But irrigation has been a mixed blessing; it has also caused waterlogging and salinity in some places. In an attempt to correct this problem, the Pakistan government, with the financial support of such international agencies as the World Bank, constructed the Left Bank Outfall Drain (LBOD) in the 1980s and '90s. The intent was to build a large artificial waterway roughly east of and parallel to the Indus to carry salt water from the plains of Punjab and Sind (Sindh) provinces to the Arabian Sea coast in the Badin region of southeastern Sind. The final segment of the LBOD consisted of building a "tidal drain" 26 miles (42 km) to the sea. However, instead of draining salt water away, the improperly designed tidal drain produced an environmental disaster in southeastern Sind: large portions of the land and freshwater lakes and ponds were flooded by salt water, crops were ruined, and freshwater fisheries were destroyed. The tidal drain issue was further complicated by instances of severe weather in the coastal region, including a destructive tropical cyclone in 1999 and torrential rains there and in Balochistan in 2007 both of which caused many deaths and forced the evacuation of tens of thousands of people. After the 2007 storms, the people of Badin called on the government to cease using the LBOD.

The Sulaiman piedmont is different from the Himalayan piedmont in that it is generally dry. Seamed with numerous streams and wadis, the surface is undulating. The gradient of the streams is comparatively steep, the floodplains are narrow, and the right bank of the Indus sometimes rises just above the main channel.

The lower Indus plain, the course of which goes through Sind province, is flat, with a gradient as slight as 1 foot per 3 miles (1 metre per 10 km). The micro relief is quite similar to that of the upper Indus plain. The valley of the Indus and its banks have risen higher than the surrounding land as a result of the aggradational work of the river; and though the river is lined with flood-protecting bunds along its course, the alluvial sands and clays of the soil tend to give way before floods, leading the river to change course frequently. The level surface of the plain is disturbed at Sukkur and Hyderabad, where there are random outcroppings of limestone. The Indus delta has its apex near Thatta, below which distributaries of the river spread out to form the deltaic plain. To the southeast of that point is the Rann of Kachchh (Kutch), which is an expanse of saline marsh. The coastal tract is low and flat, except where the Pabbi Hills meet the coast between Karachi and Ras Muari (Cape Monze).

Manchhar, a marshy lake west of the Indus, has an area of 14 square miles (36 square km) at low water but extends for no less than 200 square miles (500 square km) when full; on such occasions it is one of the largest freshwater lakes in South Asia. The quality of groundwater in the Indus plain varies, that in the southern zone (Sind) being mostly saline and unfit for agricultural use. Extensive areas in both the northern and southern zones of the plain have been affected by waterlogging and salinity. In the south the Indus delta (in marked contrast to the Ganges-Brahmaputra delta) is a wild waste. When high tides and Indus floods coincide, the littoral is flooded for some 20 miles (30 km) inland.

The desert areas

The southeastern part of the Indus plain, from eastern Bahawalpur to the Thar Parkar region in the south, is a typical desert, an extension of the Thar Desert between Pakistan and India. It is separated from the central irrigated zone of the plains by the dry bed of the Ghaggar River in Bahawalpur and the eastern Nara Canal in Sind. The desert is variously known as the Cholistan or Rohi Desert in Bahawalpur and the Pat or Thar Desert in Sind. The surface of the desert is a wild maze of sand dunes and sand ridges. Most of the Sind Sagar Doab, the most western of the doabs of Punjab, was an unproductive wasteland (known as the Thal Desert) before the construction of the Jinnah Barrage on the Indus River near Kalabagh in 1946. The Thal canal system, which draws water from the barrage, has turned parts of the desert into fertile cultivated land.

Soils

Pakistan's soils are classified as pedocals, which comprise a dry soil group with high concentrations of calcium carbonate and a low content of organic matter; they are characteristic of a land with low and erratic precipitation. The major soil groupings are Indus basin soils, mountain soils, and sandy desert soils. However, the very mode of soil formation gives rise to their diversification even within small areas. These soils vary in texture, chemical composition, colour, and organic content from place to place.

The Indus basin soils are mostly thick alluvium deposited by rivers and are of recent origin. Soils in the vicinity of river courses are the most recent and vary in texture from sand to silt loam and silty clay loams. They have a low organic content and are collectively known as the khaddar soils. Away from the river, toward the middle of the doabs, older alluvial soils (called bangar) are widely distributed. These soils are medium to fine in texture, have low organic content, and are highly productive under conditions of irrigation and fertilization. In some waterlogged areas, however, these soils are salinized. Strongly alkaline soils are localized in some small patches. In the submontane areas under subhumid conditions these soils are noncalcareous and have slightly higher organic content. In the delta the estuarine soils are excessively saline and barren.

Mountain soils are both residual (i.e., formed in a stationary position) and transported. Shallow residual soils have developed along the slopes and in the broken hill country. Those soils generally are strongly calcareous and have low organic content, but under subhumid conditions their organic content increases.

Sandy desert soils cover the Cholistan part of Sind Sagar Doab and western Balochistan. They include both shifting sandy soils and clayey floodplain soils. These include moderately calcareous and eolian (wind-borne) soils.

Climate

Aridity is the most pervasive aspect of Pakistan's climate, and its continental nature can be seen in the extremes of temperature. Pakistan is situated on the edge of a monsoonal (i.e., wet-dry) system. Precipitation throughout the country generally is erratic, and its volume is highly variable. The rainy monsoon winds, the exact margins of which vary from year to year, blow in intermittent bursts, and most moisture comes in the summer. Tropical storms from the Arabian Sea provide precipitation to the coastal areas but are also variable in character.

The efficiency of the monsoonal precipitation is poor, because of its concentration from early July to mid-September, when high temperatures maximize loss through evaporation. In the north the mean annual precipitation at Peshawar is 13 inches (330 mm), and at Rawalpindi it reaches 37 inches (950 mm). In the plains, however, mean annual precipitation generally decreases from northeast to southwest, falling from about 20 inches (500 mm) at Lahore to less than 5 inches (130 mm) in the Indus River corridor and 3.5 inches (90 mm) at Sukkur. Under maritime influence, precipitation increases slightly to about 6 inches (155 mm) at Hyderabad and 8 inches (200 mm) at Karachi.

The 20-inch (500-mm) precipitation line, which runs northwest from near Lahore, marks off the Potwar Plateau and a part of the Indus plain in the northeast; these areas receive enough rainfall for dry farming (farming without irrigation). South of this region, cultivation is confined mainly to riverine strips until the advent of irrigation. Most of the Balochistan plateau, especially in the west and south, is exceptionally dry.

Pakistan's continental type of climate is characterized by extreme variations of temperature, both seasonally and daily. High elevations modify the climate in the cold, snow-covered northern mountains; temperatures on the Balochistan plateau are somewhat higher. Along the coastal strip, the climate is modified by sea breezes. In the rest of the country, temperatures reach great extremes in the summer; the mean temperature during June is 100 °F (38 °C) in the plains, where the highest temperatures can exceed 117 °F (47 °C). Jacobabad, in Sind, has recorded the highest temperature in Pakistan, 127 °F (53 °C). In the summer, hot winds called loos blow across the plains during the day. Trees shed their leaves to avoid excessive moisture loss. The dry, hot weather is broken occasionally by dust storms and thunderstorms that temporarily lower the temperature. Evenings are cool; the diurnal variation in temperature may be as much as 20 to 30 °F (11 to 17 °C). Winters are cold, with minimum mean temperatures of about 40 °F (4 °C) in January.

Plant and animal life

Differences of latitude, elevation, soil type, and climate have favoured a variety of plant growth. Drought-resistant vegetation in the desert consists of stunted thorny scrub, mostly acacia. The plains present a parkland view of scattered trees. Dry scrub forests, called rakhs, grow in parts of the arid plain. In the northern and northwestern foothills and plains, shrub forests, principally acacia, and wild olive are found. In the wetter parts of the northern and northwestern mountains, evergreen coniferous softwood forests, with some broad-leaved species, grow. Fir, deodar, blue pine (Pinus wallichiana), and spruce are the principal coniferous trees. At lower elevations, below 3,000 feet (900 metres), broad-leaved oaks, maples, birches, walnuts, and chestnuts predominate. Conifers are an important source of commercial timber. In the arid landscape of the Potwar Plateau, some hills are only thinly wooded. In the northern ranges of the Balochistan plateau are some groves of pine and olive. The babul tree (Acacia arabica) is common in the Indus River valley, as are many species of fruit trees. The country's forest cover is naturally sparse, but it has been diminished further by excessive timber cutting and overgrazing.

Destruction of natural habitats and excessive hunting have led to a reduction in the range of animal life in large parts of the country, but wildlife can still be found in abundance in some areas. The variety of large mammals in the northern mountains includes brown bears, Asiatic black bears (Ursus thibetanus, also known as the Himalayan bear), leopards, rare snow leopards, Siberian ibex (Capra ibex sibirica), and wild sheep, including markhors, Marco Polo sheep (Ovis ammon polii, a type of argali), and Chiltan wild goats (Capra aegagrus chialtanensis).

Manchhar Lake in Sind has many aquatic birds, including mallards, teals, shovelers, spoonbills, geese, pochards, and wood ducks. Crocodiles, gavials (crocodile-like reptiles), pythons, and wild boars inhabit the Indus River delta area. The Indus River itself is home to the Indus river dolphin, a freshwater dolphin whose habitat has been severely stressed by hunting, pollution, and the creation of dams and barrages. At least two types of sea turtles, the green and olive ridley, nest on the Makran coast.

Desert gazelles are widely distributed, including nilgais, chinkaras (Gazella gazella bennetti), and muntjacs. Jackals, foxes, and various wild cats (including Eurasian lynxes, caracals, fishing cats, and jungle cats [Felis chaus]) are also found throughout the country. Despite occasional reported sightings of the Asiatic cheetah, that species is likely extinct in Pakistan. A series of national parks and game preserves was established beginning in the 1970s. However, a number of species have been declared endangered, including the Indus river dolphin, snow leopard, and gavial.

People

Ethnic composition

The area currently occupied by Pakistan has long been a route of military conquest and an entrepôt for peoples and cultures. It is therefore a significant cultural and ethnic melting pot. Modern Pakistan's population can be divided broadly into five major and several minor ethnic groups. The Punjabis, who constitute roughly half of the population, are the single largest group. The Pashtuns (Pathans) account for about one-eighth of the population, and Sindhis form a somewhat smaller group. Of the remaining population, the muhajirs Muslims who fled to Pakistan after the partition in 1947 and Balochs constitute the largest groups.

There are subgroups within each of these five categories, as well as a number of smaller ethnic groups not included among them. The Arains, Rajputs, and Jats all Punjabis regard themselves as ethnically distinct. Some groups overlap the five categories; for instance, there are Punjabi Pashtuns as well as Hazarvi Pashtuns. Some smaller groups, such as the Brahuis in Sindh (Sind) and the Siraikis in Punjab, are also ethnically distinct. Tribal Pashtuns are another subgroup of the Pashtun constellation. Divided into numerous tribal orders, they inhabit the mountainous region along the Afghan frontier. Among these are the Yusufzai, Orakzai, Swati, Afridi, Wazir, Mohmand, and Mahsud. Other unique tribal peoples are found still farther north in the remoter mountain regions of Dir, Chitral, Hunza, and Gilgit.

Linguistic composition

Pakistan is, in general, linguistically heterogeneous, and no single language can be said to be common to the whole population. Each of its principal languages has a strong regional focus, although statistics show some languages to be distributed between various provinces because administrative boundaries cut across linguistic regions. The picture is also complicated by the fact that, especially in Sindh, there are substantial numbers of Urdu- and Punjabi-speaking muhajirs. In addition to Urdu and Punjabi, other languages claimed as mother tongues include Sindhi, Pashto, Siraiki, Balochi, and Brahui.

Having originated during the Mughal period (early 16th to mid-18th century), Urdu is the youngest of the country's languages and is not indigenous to Pakistan. It is similar to Hindi, the most widely spoken language of India. Although the two languages have a common base, in its literary form Urdu emphasizes words of Persian and Arabic origin, whereas Hindi emphasizes words of Sanskrit origin. Urdu is written in a modified version of the Persian script, whereas Hindi is written in Devanagari script. Because it is predominantly the language of the educated Muslims of northern India, including the Punjab, Urdu has strong associations with Muslim nationalism hence the ideological significance of Urdu in Pakistani politics. Urdu is the mother tongue of only a small proportion of the population of Pakistan, but it is the country's only official language; it is taught in the schools along with the regional languages.

The 1956 constitution prescribed the use of English (the administrative language during the colonial period) for official purposes for 20 years, and the 1962 constitution made that use indefinite. The 1973 constitution, however, designated a 15-year transition period to Urdu, after which English would no longer be used for official purposes. That provision of the constitution has not been fully implemented. English is still taught and used in schools at all levels, and it remains the lingua franca of the government, intelligentsia, and military. With the exception of this educated elite, English is spoken fluently by only a small percentage of the population. Many English words and phrases, however, have worked their way into local parlance, and most Pakistanis with even a modest education have some grasp of the language.

Urdu, rather than Punjabi, is the first language taught in virtually all schools in Punjab province, so every educated Punjabi reads and writes Urdu. In Pakistan, Punjabi is mainly spoken rather than written, and it is a predominantly rural rather than urban language. A movement to promote the Punjabi language began in the 1980s, and some Punjabi literature has been published using the Urdu script; among the works published are Punjabi classics that have hitherto been available in Gurmukhi script (in which Punjabi is written in India) or preserved in oral tradition.

Sindhi is derived from the Virachada dialect of the Prakrit languages. It has fewer dialects than Punjabi and is written in a special variant of the Arabic script. Prior to the partition of India in 1947, most of the educated middle class in Sindh were Hindu, and their departure to India at that time had a traumatic effect on Sindhi culture. Vigorous efforts were therefore directed toward recovering and preserving the rich Sindhi literary and cultural heritage. Large numbers of Urdu-speaking refugees settled in Sindh and came to constitute the majority of the population of its larger towns. As a consequence, the movement for the promotion of Sindhi language and culture was sometimes expressed as opposition toward Urdu. The Sindhi population feared that their language and culture would be overrun by the language and culture of the predominantly Urdu-speaking muhajir community, and that fear led to what became known as the language riots of 1972 and to the national government's decision to grant special status to the Sindhi language. (The rise of militant ethnic politics in Sindh that began in the 1980s notably the clashes between native Sindhis and organized members of the muhajir community likely can be traced to that decision.)

Pashto, the language of the Pashtuns of Khyber Pakhtunkhwa and the Federally Administered Tribal Areas, has a scant literary tradition, although it has a rich oral tradition. There are three major dialect patterns within which the various individual dialects may be classified: Northern Pashto (Pakhto), which is the variety spoken along the Afghanistan border and in and around Peshawar; Central Pashto, also called Waziri and Bannochi, spoken in Waziristan, Bannu, and Karak; and Southern Pashto, spoken in Balochistan and Quetta. As in the Punjab, Urdu is the language taught in schools, and educated Pashtuns read and write Urdu. Again, as in the case of Punjabi, there was a movement for developing the written language in Persian script and increasing the usage of Pashto.

Siraiki, also spelled Saraiki or Seraiki, is spoken in Central Pakistan from Mianwali, Punjab, to Khairpur, Sindh, and extends into Balochistan and Khyber Pakhtunkhwa as well. It is linguistically intermediate between Sindhi and Punjabi.

The two main spoken languages of Balochistan are Balochi and Brahui. An important dialect of Balochi, called Makrani or Southern Balochi, is spoken in Makran, the southern region of Balochistan, which borders Iran.

Religion

Almost all of the people of Pakistan are Muslims or at least follow Islamic traditions, and Islamic ideals and practices suffuse virtually all parts of Pakistani life. Most Pakistanis belong to the Sunni sect, the major branch of Islam. There are also significant numbers of Shī'ite

Muslims. Among Sunnis, Sufism is extremely popular and influential. In addition to the two main groups there is a very small sect called the Aḥmadiyyah, which is also sometimes called the Qadiani (for Qadian, India, where the sect originated).

The role of religion in Pakistani society and politics finds its most visible expression in the Islamic Assembly (Jamāʿat-i Islāmī) party. Founded in 1941 by Abū al-Aʿlā Mawdūdī (Maududi), one of the world's foremost thinkers in Sunni revivalism, the party has long played a role in Pakistan's political life and has continually advocated refashioning Pakistan as a chaste Islamic or theocratic state.

The majority of Pakistani Sunnis belong to the Ḥanafiyyah (Hanafite) school, which is one of four major schools (madhhabs) or subsects of Islamic jurisprudence; it is perhaps the most liberal of the four but nevertheless is still demanding in its instructions to the faithful. Two popular reform movements founded in northern India the Deoband and Barelwi schools are likewise widespread in Pakistan. Differences between the two movements over a variety of theological issues are significant to the point that violence often has erupted between them. Another group, Tablīghī Jamāʿat (founded 1926), headquartered in Raiwind, near Lahore, is a lay ministry group whose annual conference attracts hundreds of thousands of members from throughout the world. It is perhaps the largest grassroots Muslim organization in the world.

The Wahhābī movement, founded in Arabia, has made inroads in Pakistan, most notably among the tribal Pashtuns in the Afghan border areas. Moreover, after the Soviet invasion of Afghanistan in 1979, Saudi Arabia assisted Pakistan in caring for vast numbers of Afghan refugees in the border areas and in the construction and staffing of thousands of traditional Sunni madrasahs (religious schools). Those schools generally provided instruction along Wahhābī lines, and they subsequently became vehicles for the spreading influence of extremist groups (particularly al-Qaeda and the Taliban of Afghanistan) in Balochistan, Khyber Pakhtunkhwa, and elsewhere throughout the country. Although extremism in the name of Islam has become more pronounced in Pakistan since 2000, more-moderate Sunni Muslims are found in the country's business community, especially among Gujarati Memons and Chiniotis from Punjab who follow less-conservative Islamic traditions.

Among the Shīʿites there are several subsects; notable are the Ismāʿīlīs (or Seveners) including the Nizārīs (followers of the Aga Khans, among whom are the Khojas and the Bohrās), who are prominent in commerce and industry and the Ithnā ʿAshariyyah (or Twelvers), who are more austere in their practices and more closely resemble the Shīʿite tradition found in Iran. Shīʿites have long been the target of Sunni radicals, and violent encounters between followers of the two sects are common.

With the exception of some sects, such as Dawoodi Bohrās, there is no concept of an ordained priesthood among Pakistan's Muslims. Anyone who leads prayers in mosques may be appointed imam. Those who are formally trained in religion are accorded the honorific mullah or mawlānā. Collectively, the community of Muslim scholars is known as the ʿulamāʾ ("scholars"), but among the practitioners of a more popular sect of Islam (generally associated with Sufism) there are powerful hereditary networks of holy men called pīrs, who receive great reverence (as well as gifts in cash or kind) from a multitude of followers. An established pīr may pass on his spiritual powers and sanctified authority to one or more of his murīds ("disciples"), who may then operate as pīrs in their own right. There are also many self-appointed pīrs who practice locally without being properly inducted into one of the major Sufi orders. Pīrs who occupy high positions in the pīr hierarchy wield great power and play an influential role in public affairs.

Among the basic tenets of the Aḥmadiyyah is the belief that other prophets came after Muhammad and that their leader, the 19th century's Mīrzā Ghulām Aḥmad, was called to accept a divine mission. The Aḥmadiyyah therefore appear to question Muhammad's role as the last of God's prophets. More conservative Muslims find this seeming revision of traditional belief blasphemous, and in 1974 a constitutional amendment declared the Aḥmadiyyah community to be non-Muslims. The community became the focal point of riots in the Punjab in 1953, instigated by the Islamic Assembly but also including a broad representation of religious groups. Since then the Aḥmadiyyah have experienced considerable persecution, particularly during the administration (1977–88) of Gen. Mohammad Zia ul-Haq when they were denied all semblance of Islamic character and they have been denied positions in the civil service and the military and often have been forced to conceal their identity.

At the time of partition, most Hindus left newly formed West Pakistan for India. In the east, wealthier Hindus also fled newly formed East Pakistan, but a sizeable minority of Hindus (nearly 10 million) stayed behind. The vast majority remained there until the civil war of 1971 (which led to the creation of Bangladesh) compelled them to seek refuge in India.

There is also a small but fairly significant population of Christians in the country. There are adherents to a variety of denominations, Roman Catholicism being the largest. Violent attacks against Christians became increasingly common during the Zia ul-Haq regime, a trend that continued afterward with the increase of religious strife.

Settlement patterns

Geographically, the population of Pakistan is distributed rather unevenly. More than half of the population is in Punjab; on the other hand, Balochistan, the largest province in terms of area, has significant areas with virtually no settled population. Likewise, within each province, the population further pools in various areas. Much of the population of Balochistan, for instance, is concentrated in the area of Quetta. The region around Karachi and the inhabited strip along the Indus River are the most densely settled areas in Sindh province. Within Punjab the population density generally decreases from northeast to southwest. In Khyber Pakhtunkhwa the plain around Peshawar and Mardan is a high-density area. Broadly speaking, population density is greatest in fertile agricultural areas. Nomadism and transhumance, once common lifestyles in Pakistan, are practiced by relatively few people in the 21st century.

Traditional regions

The traditional regions of Pakistan, shaped by ecological factors and historical evolution, are reflected in the administrative division of the country into the four provinces of Sindh, Punjab, Khyber Pakhtunkhwa (including the Federally Administered Tribal Areas), and Balochistan, each of which is ethnically and linguistically distinct.

In the Punjab, until the advent of irrigation, most of the population was restricted to those areas receiving more than 20 inches (500 mm) of precipitation annually, namely the Potwar Plateau and the upper Indus plain. Such areas where dry farming is practiced are referred to as barani. Later, large areas of uncultivated land in the Indus River plain of the southern Punjab were irrigated by canals and populated by colonists drawn from other parts of the province. Referred to as the Canal Colony, that area now forms the richest agricultural region of the country.

Agricultural wealth is concentrated in those barani areas around Lahore that have benefited from irrigation, together with the Canal Colony areas and Sindh province. Those regions contain most of the rural population of Pakistan and produce more than half of the country's wheat and virtually all of its cotton and rice. Landholdings are larger in the Canal Colony areas of the Punjab and in Sindh.

Elsewhere, in the overpopulated and poor districts of the barani region that do not benefit from irrigation, holdings are exceedingly small and fragmented. In those districts, there is great pressure to migrate from the villages in order to find employment in towns, to enlist in the armed forces, or to seek work abroad, particularly in the Persian Gulf states of the Middle East.

Rural settlement

About two-thirds of the rural population of Pakistan lives in nucleated villages or hamlets (i.e., in compact groups of dwellings). Sometimes, as is generally the case in Khyber Pakhtunkhwa, the houses are placed in a ring with windowless outer walls, so that each complex resembles a protected fortress with a few guarded entrances. Dispersed habitation patterns in the form of isolated single homesteads are rare, occurring only in a few mountainous areas. But it is not uncommon to find numerous satellite hamlets of varying sizes near larger villages; such hamlets are occupied either by a landlord (along with his family, servants, and sharecroppers) or else by members of an extended family group living together in adjoining houses. The spread of tube wells (driven wells) in the Punjab has increased the tendency for such dispersal, for people often prefer to live near their tube wells in order to guard the valuable machinery. The concept of village, therefore, often tends to be equivalent to that of the mawza' (an area of land that, together with a village and its satellite hamlets, forms a unit in land-revenue records). It is difficult to speak of an average size of village, for patterns of habitation are complex. Most groups of dwellings have a minimum of a dozen or a score of houses, and there are usually a few hundred dwellings in each "village." Large villages rarely have populations exceeding 2,500 persons.

Three basic types of village layout are to be found. Most of the older settlements are of the "spiderweb" form, having at least one focal point, such as the village mosque, some shops, or a well from which lanes radiate. A few villages follow the contours of hill slopes and other natural features. In the Canal Colony areas, villages are of a regular rectangular pattern, with a well, a mosque, and a school, as well as the house of the village headman, at the centre and with the houses being arranged in a series of concentric rectangles. Houses are built from available local materials; the vast majority are of adobe, a material that is not only cheap and reasonably durable in the dry climate but also provides better insulation from extremes of heat and cold than brick or stone. Houses usually have walled courtyards where animals are tethered and where people sleep in the open in the hot summer.

Urban settlement

The urban population of Pakistan represents about two-fifths of the total. Two cities have a dominating position Karachi, the capital of Sindh province (and of the country until 1959), and Lahore, the capital of Punjab. Since the 1960s, government policy has been directed toward the dispersal of industry, which had become heavily concentrated in Karachi. As a consequence, urban growth has been more evenly distributed among several cities. Karachi remains the principal port and centre of commerce and industry.

Rapid and unplanned urban expansion has been paralleled by a deterioration in living conditions, particularly in the housing conditions of lower-income groups. Many urban households are unable to pay rent for the cheapest form of available housing and live in shacks in makeshift communities known collectively as katchi abadis. Water supply and sewerage systems are inadequate, and in many areas residents have to share communal water taps. Inadequate urban transport is also a major problem.

Karachi experienced serious ethnic conflict between the muhajir immigrants and Sindhis and (since the late 1980s) between the Sindhis and Punjabis. Discouraged by civil strife, businesses both industrial and commercial began to relocate to Punjab, particularly in and around Lahore. After Karachi and Lahore, the principal cities are Faisalabad and Rawalpindi in Punjab and Peshawar, the capital of Khyber Pakhtunkhwa. Quetta is the capital and largest city of Balochistan. The national capital, Islamabad, adjoins Rawalpindi.

Demographic trends

Pakistan is one of the most populous countries in the world. Infant mortality has decreased, and life expectancy has increased; nearly two-thirds of the population is under 30 years of age. The birth rate is higher than the world's average, while the death rate is lower. Life expectancy is 66 years for men and 70 years for women.

The overwhelming demographic fact of Pakistani history is the enormous shift of population during the country's partition from India. Millions of Hindus and Sikhs left Pakistan, and about eight million immigrants (muhajirs) then roughly one-fourth of the country's population arrived from India, bringing their own language (mostly Urdu), culture, and identity. Most settled in Sindh province, but muhajir pockets can be found throughout the country.

The major demographic shifts in the postindependence period have been movements within the country (largely to urban areas), the exodus of large numbers of Pakistanis to live and work abroad, and the influx of large numbers of Afghan refugees into the country beginning in the early 1980s.

The movement of people to urban areas and abroad can be tied to an overall increase in population which has strained resources, particularly in rural areas largely due to improved health care and dietary intake. The economies of most parts of the countryside have been unable to absorb the increased population, and many Pakistanis have turned to the cities in search of jobs. Though Karachi and Lahore are the only two cities that can properly be called megalopolises, all of the cities of Pakistan have grown rapidly in size and population since independence. Even in the cities, however, resources have been strained. Beginning in the oil boom of the 1970s, large numbers of Pakistanis traveled to the Persian Gulf states seeking work. Most found employment as unskilled labourers, traveling without their families and returning home at the end of their contracted time. Also, a great many Pakistanis mostly among the educated professional classes emigrated to the West, either to the United States or to the United Kingdom and other Commonwealth countries, but with advances in modern communications they often have kept in close contact with other family members still in Pakistan.

During the 1980s millions of Afghans fled to Pakistan during the Afghan War. Most of them settled along the two countries' shared border, although a significant number migrated to larger cities. It was only with the Soviet withdrawal from Afghanistan in the late 1980s and, more importantly, the end of Taliban rule there in 2001 that significant numbers of Afghans were repatriated. Nevertheless, a great many have remained in refugee camps in the border areas as well as in Pakistan's cities.

Economy

After several experiments in economic restructuring, Pakistan currently operates a mixed economy in which state-owned enterprises account for a large portion of gross domestic product (GDP). The country has experimented with several economic models during its existence. At first, Pakistan's economy was largely based on private enterprise, but significant sectors of it were nationalized beginning in the early 1970s, including financial services, manufacturing, and transportation. Further changes were made in the 1980s, under the military government of Zia ul-Haq. Specifically, an "Islamic" economy was introduced, which outlawed practices forbidden by Sharī'ah (Muslim law) e.g., charging interest on loans (ribā) and mandated such traditional religious practices as the payment of zakāt (tithe) and 'ushr (land tax). Though portions of the Islamic economy have remained in place, the state began in the 1990s to privatize in whole or in part large sectors of the nationalized economy.

The economy, which was primarily agricultural at the time of independence, has become considerably diversified. Agriculture, now no longer the largest sector, contributes roughly one-fifth of GDP, while manufacturing provides about one-sixth. Trade and services, which combined constitute the largest component of the economy, have grown considerably. In terms of the structure of its economy, Pakistan resembles the middle-income countries of East and Southeast Asia more than the poorer countries of the Indian subcontinent. Economic performance compares favourably with that of many other developing countries; Pakistan has maintained a sustained and fairly steady annual growth rate since independence.

At the same time, there has been a relentless increase in population, so, despite real growth in the economy, output per capita has risen only slowly. This slow growth in per capita income has not coincided with a high incidence of absolute poverty, however, which has been considerably smaller in Pakistan than in other South Asian countries. Nonetheless, a significant proportion of the population lives below the poverty line, and the relative prosperity of the industrialized regions around Karachi and Lahore contrasts sharply with the poverty of the Punjab's barani areas, the semiarid Balochistan, Khyber Pakhtunkhwa, and the Federally Administered Tribal Areas.

Agriculture, forestry, and fishing

Overall, approximately one-fourth of Pakistan is arable land, although only small fractions of that are in permanent crops (about 1 percent) or permanent pastures (6 percent). Roughly 5 percent of the country is forested. Nonetheless, agriculture, forestry, and fishing still provide employment for the single largest proportion of the labour force and a livelihood for an even larger segment of the population. Land-reform programs implemented in 1959, 1972, and 1977 began to deal with the problems of large-scale, often absentee ownership of land and the excessive fragmentation of small holdings by introducing maximum and minimum area limits. The commercialization of agriculture has also resulted in fairly large-scale transfers of land, concentrating its ownership among middle-class farmers.

The attention given to the agricultural sector in development plans has brought about some radical changes in centuries-old farming techniques. The construction of tube wells for irrigation and salinity control, the use of chemical fertilizers and scientifically selected seeds, and the gradual introduction of farm machinery have all contributed to the notable increase in productivity. As a consequence, Pakistan experienced what became known as the Green Revolution during the late 1960s, leaving a surplus that was partly shipped to East Pakistan (Bangladesh) and partly exported; self-sufficiency in wheat the national staple was achieved by about 1970. Cotton production also rose, which added to the domestic production of textiles and edible cottonseed oils. Rice is the second major food staple and one of the country's important export crops. Large domestic sugar subsidies have been primarily responsible for an increase in sugarcane production. Other crops include chickpeas, pearl millet (bajra), corn (maize), rapeseed, and mustard, as well as a variety of garden crops, including onions, peppers, and potatoes. Pakistan benefits greatly from having two growing seasons, rabi (spring harvest) and kharif (fall harvest).

The cultivation and transportation of illicit narcotics remains a large sector of the informal economy. Pakistan is one of the world's leading producers of opium poppy (for the production of heroin) and also produces or transports cannabis (as hashish) from Afghanistan for local markets and for reexport abroad.

Animal husbandry provides important domestic and export products. Livestock includes cattle, buffalo, sheep, goats, camels, and poultry. These animals provide meat and dairy products for local consumption, as well as wool for the carpet industry and for export and hides and skins for the leather industry. The contribution of forestry to national income remains negligible, but that of fisheries has risen. Fishing activity is centred in Karachi, and part of the catch of lobster and other shellfish is exported.

River water is used in large parts of the country to irrigate agricultural areas. The Balochistan plateau has a remarkable indigenous method of irrigation called the qanāt (or kārīz) system, which consists of underground channels and galleries that collect subsoil water at the foot of hills and carry it to fields and villages. The water is drawn from the channels through shafts that are sunk into the fields at suitable intervals. Because the channels are underground, the loss of water by evaporation is minimized.

Resources and power

Minerals

The exploration of Pakistan's mineral wealth is far from complete, but some two dozen different types of exploitable minerals have been located. Iron ore deposits are mostly of poor quality. The most extensive known reserves are situated in the Kalabagh region, in western Punjab. Other low-grade ore reserves have been found in Hazara, in Khyber Pakhtunkhwa. Small reserves of high-grade iron ore have been identified in Chitral and in the Chilghazi area (located in northwestern Balochistan), as well as in Khyber Pakhtunkhwa. Deposits of copper ore equaling or surpassing the reserves of iron ore have been found, but most sites remain unexploited. There are enormous reserves of easily exploited limestone that form the basis of a growing cement industry, a major component of the manufacturing sector. Other minerals that are exploited include chromite (mostly for export), barite, celestine (strontium sulfate), antimony, aragonite (calcium carbonate), gypsum, rock salt, and marble and granite.

Hydrocarbons and power

Pakistan has modest quantities of petroleum and some large natural gas fields. The first oil discovery was made in 1915. Pakistan intensified the search for oil and natural gas in the 1980s and was rewarded with the discovery of a number of new oil fields in the Potwar Plateau region and in Sind. A number of fields have been developed, particularly near Badin, in Sind. Despite the continued search for new and richer fields (including some offshore exploration and drilling), Pakistan has had to import increasing amounts of oil from abroad to satisfy growing consumption, making the country vulnerable to fluctuations in world oil markets. Most imports take the form of crude oil, which is refined into various products. Pakistan's refinery capacity well exceeds its domestic crude production. The oil sector is regulated by the Ministry of Petroleum and Natural Resources, and international oil companies are authorized to operate in Pakistan in cooperation with domestic companies.

The largest natural gas deposits are at Sui (on the border between Balochistan and Punjab), discovered in 1953. A smaller field, at Mari, in northeast Sind province, was found in 1957. A number of smaller natural gas fields subsequently have been discovered in various areas. A network of gas pipelines links the fields with the main consumption areas: Karachi, Lahore, Multan, Faisalabad, and Islamabad. Although proven reserves are large, they have not kept pace with domestic consumption.

Coal mining is one of the country's oldest industries. The quality of the coal is poor, and the mines have been worked below capacity because of the difficulty of access; despite ample reserves, the country regularly imports coal.

Although energy production has grown faster than the economy as a whole, it has not kept pace with demand, and as a result there are shortages of fuel and electric power. The bulk of power requirements are provided by thermal plants (coal, oil, and natural gas), with most of the remainder provided by hydroelectric installations.

The generation, transmission, and distribution of power is the responsibility of the Pakistani Water and Power Development Authority (WAPDA), a public-sector corporation. WAPDA lost its monopoly over generation after Pakistan entered into an agreement in 1989 with a consortium of foreign firms to produce power from giant oil-fired plants located at Hub, near Karachi; the plants were completed in 1997.

Great progress, however, has been made in the development of the hydroelectric potential of Pakistan's rivers. A giant hydroelectric plant is in operation at the Mangla Dam, on the Jhelum River in Azad Kashmir (the part of Kashmir under Pakistani administration). Another such source is the giant Tarbela Dam, on the Indus River.

Pakistan has three nuclear power plants, the Karachi Nuclear Power Plant (completed 1972), the Chashma Nuclear Power Plant-1 (2000), and the Chashma Nuclear Power Plant-2 (2011). The Chashma plants are at Kundian, Punjab. Nuclear power provides only a tiny proportion of the country's total energy production.

Manufacturing

Mining and quarrying account for a small percentage of GDP and of total employment. Manufacturing, however, constitutes a healthy proportion. The beginning of the main industrialization effort dates to the cessation of trade between India and Pakistan in 1949, soon after the two countries gained independence. Initially it was based on the processing of raw agricultural materials for domestic consumption and for export. This led to the construction of cotton textile mills a development that now accounts for a large part of the total employment in industry. Woolen textiles, sugar, paper, tobacco, and leather industries also provide many jobs for the industrial labour force.

The growing trade deficit in the mid-1950s compelled the government to cut down on imports, which encouraged the establishment of a number of import-substitution industries. At first these factories produced mainly consumer goods, but gradually they came to produce intermediate goods and a range of capital goods, including chemicals, fertilizers, and light engineering products. Nevertheless, Pakistan still has to import a large proportion of the capital equipment and raw materials required by industry. In the 1970s and early '80s Pakistan set up an integrated iron and steel mill at Pipri, near Karachi, with the financial and technical assistance of the Soviet Union. A new port, Port Qāsim (officially Port Muḥammad Bin Qāsim), was built to bring iron ore and coal for the mill.

Initially Karachi was the centre of Pakistan's industrialization effort, but in the late 1960s and early '70s Lahore and the cities around it began to industrialize rapidly. Karachi's ethnic problems in the late 1980s and early '90s accelerated this process, and Punjab increasingly became Karachi's competitor in industrial output.

Major manufactured products include jute and cotton textiles, cement, vegetable ghee, cigarettes, and bicycles. Although the country still imports most of its motor vehicles, some Pakistani firms have entered into contracts with foreign companies to produce automobiles, motorcycles, and industrial tractors domestically.

Finance

Finance contributes a relatively small value to GDP, though its growth rate in the late 20th and early 21st centuries has been considerable. Pakistan has a variety of state banks, state-run banks (though more-recent trends have been toward privatizing these), scheduled (i.e., commercial) banks, private banks, and foreign banks. Noteworthy has been the spread of banks that operate within the principles of Islamic law. A number of such institutions were established beginning in the 1980s, and, more recently, several established Western-style banks have opened up divisions offering Islamic banking services.

Pakistan has a fairly well-developed system of financial services. The State Bank of Pakistan (1948) has overall control of the banking sector, acts as banker to the central and provincial governments, and administers official monetary and credit policies, including exchange controls. It has the sole right to issue currency (the Pakistani rupee) and has custody of the country's gold and foreign-exchange reserves.

Pakistan has a number of commercial banks, called scheduled banks, which are subject to strict State Bank requirements as to paid-up capital and reserves. They account for the bulk of total deposits, collected through a network of branch offices. A few specialist financial institutions provide medium- and long-term credit for industrial, agricultural, and housing purposes and include the Pakistan Industrial Credit and Investment Corporation (1957; since 2001, PICIC Commercial Bank, Ltd.), the Industrial Development Bank of Pakistan (1961), the Agricultural Development Bank of Pakistan (1961), and the House Building Finance Corporation (1952). There are a number of private banks, many of which operate from Karachi. Habib Bank, Ltd., is one of the oldest. The Bank of Credit and Commerce International (BCCI) was founded in Pakistan in 1972; BCCI's collapse in 1991 precipitated a major international banking scandal.

The Karachi Stock Exchange (Guarantee) Limited (1947), Lahore Stock Exchange (Guarantee) Limited (1970), and Islamabad Stock Exchange (Guarantee) Limited (1989) are the largest such institutions in the country; each deals in stocks and shares of registered companies. The Investment Corporation of Pakistan (1966) and the National Investment Trust (1962) were founded by the state to help channel domestic savings into the capital market; both have since been partly privatized. As part of the development of the "Islamic" economy, interest-free banking and financing practices have been instituted in many specialized banks.

Trade

Trade has grown into one of the major sectors of the Pakistani economy and employs a significant proportion of the workforce. Although there has been a trend toward increasing exports, the country has had a chronic annual trade deficit, with imports often outstripping exports. Over the years, important changes have taken place in the composition of foreign trade. In particular, while the proportion of total exports from primary commodities, including raw cotton, has fallen, the share of manufactures has greatly increased. But the bulk of the manufactured products coming into the export trade consists of cotton goods, so that Pakistan remains as dependent as ever on its leading cash crop. The other manufactures exported come mostly from industries based on agriculture, such as leather and leather goods and carpets; exports of rice and petroleum products are also important. The shift toward manufactured agricultural exports, which have a higher added-value content than primary commodities, has been encouraged by the government. The trade deficits and shortages of foreign exchange have made it necessary for the government to restrict imports and to provide financial incentives to promote export trade. Major imports consist of machinery, chemicals and chemical products, crude oil, refined petroleum, food and edible oils, and motor vehicles. Pakistan's most important trading partners are the United States, the United Arab Emirates, Saudi Arabia, Afghanistan, and China.

Services

The government has traditionally been a major employer, and, just as in other former colonial countries with a well-developed civil service, government positions are coveted for the financial security that they offer. Combined with public administration, defense, construction, and public utilities, services account for roughly one-fourth of GDP and employ about one-fifth of the workforce. Tourism traditionally has contributed little to the economy, but the country has consistently attracted a number of tourists who engage in "adventure" tours, particularly in the high mountains of the north, where the Karakoram Highway provides access to some of the loftier peaks for hikers and climbers. Likewise, the ruins at Mohenjo-daro and Taxila designated

UNESCO World Heritage sites in 1980 attract a number of interested outsiders each year.

Remittances from workers abroad constitute a large (though extremely difficult to measure) source of revenue. At any given time there are several million Pakistanis working abroad, throughout the world; officially, the income that they send home (as well as money remitted by Pakistani immigrants abroad) amounts to hundreds of millions of dollars annually. Much income is likely transferred through unofficial channels either by hand or through the services of the traditional system of money exchanges known as hawala and the total amount of money remitted from abroad is likely much higher than official statements.

Labour and taxation

The trade union movement dates to the late 19th century, but, because Pakistan's industrial sector (inherited at independence) was so small, organized labour as a proportion of total employment is still in the minority. This has not prevented it from becoming an important political force. Before the 1971 civil war, there were considerably more than 1,000 registered unions, most of them organized within individual establishments. Countrywide unions based on a common craft or a particular industry were very few. Most of the unions were situated in the urban centres and were affiliated with one of three national labour confederations. After the civil war and the emergence of Bangladesh, the number of unions declined to a few hundred, affiliated with one umbrella organization, the Pakistan National Federation of Trade Unions.

Because of the country's relatively high rates of unemployment, employers have remained in a strong position, and many of them have been able to bypass working agreements and laws. Only the unions in the larger industries (e.g., cotton textiles) have had the necessary coherence to fight back. Labour laws introduced in 1972 met some of the demands (job security, social welfare, pensions) of organized labour but also sought to control political activity by industrial workers. Labour union activity was severely constrained by the military government of 1977–88 but was subsequently revived during the first administration (1988–91) of Benazir Bhutto.

Taxation accounts for the main source of government revenue: the government levies sales taxes, income taxes, customs duties, and excise taxes. Sales and income taxes account for the largest proportion of all revenues, with nontax receipts constituting a large portion of the balance. Government expenditures exceed revenues by a large amount. Income tax rates have been comparatively high, but the tax base has been so small that individual and corporate income tax revenues have remained substantially lower than excise, sales, and other indirect taxes. The government has been able to maintain heavy expenditures on development and defense because of the inflow of foreign aid and worker remittances.

Transportation and telecommunications

Buses and trucks have displaced rail as the principal long-distance carrier. A program of deregulation of the road transport industry was undertaken in 1970 and encouraged the entry of a large number of independent operators into the sector. Trucks and tractor-drawn trailers have largely displaced the traditional bullock cart for local transport of produce to markets, but in many rural areas animal power is still crucial to economic survival. Air transport of cargo and passengers has become increasingly important.

All the main cities are connected by major highways, and Pakistan is connected to each of its neighbours, including China, by road. The great majority of roads are paved. The country's main rail route runs more than 1,000 miles (1,600 km) north from Karachi to Peshawar, via Lahore and Rawalpindi. Another main line branches northwestward from Sukkur to Quetta.

Pakistan International Airlines (PIA), established in 1954, is the national carrier; until the mid-1990s it was the sole domestic carrier, but since then a number of small regional airlines and charter services have been established. (PIA also runs international flights to Europe, the Middle East, Africa, and East Asia, as well as to neighbouring Afghanistan.) The principal airports are located at Karachi, Lahore,

Rawalpindi, Quetta, and Peshawar. Karachi, Port Qāsim, and Gwadar are the principal port cities. Since 2012 management and modernization of Gwadar's port have been handled by a Chinese state-owned firm. A number of small harbours along the Makran Coast handle the small boats that ply between Pakistan and the Persian Gulf states. In the early 1990s the limitations of the transportation system emerged as a major constraint on the modernization of the economy, prompting the government to undertake large-scale investments in the highway sector. Private entrepreneurs were invited to participate on the basis of a "build-operate-transfer" (BOT) approach, which subsequently became popular in other developing countries. (In the BOT system, private entrepreneurs build and operate infrastructure facilities such as ports, highways, and power plants and then recover their costs by charging tariffs from the users. Once the investors have recovered their outlay, the facility created is transferred to the government.)

Pakistan's telephone system has developed and expanded since the first years of independence. Since 1988 the government has stimulated investment in telecommunications and prompted the development of an efficient national system. Pakistan Telecommunications Company, Ltd. originally founded in 1947 as the state-run Pakistan Posts and Telegraph Department and partly privatized in 1994 is the country's largest carrier. Despite increasing capacity, standard telephone service is generally sparse, with only a fraction of households having a landline and rural areas generally still without any standard services. Mobile phone usage, however, has increased dramatically. Pakistani networks are connected with the outside world via satellite and by fibre-optic lines. At the beginning of the 21st century, personal computer ownership was almost nonexistent and Internet access was sparse. Since that time, however, Pakistan experienced significant growth: by the end of the decade, the proportion of households with a personal computer had grown to almost one-tenth. While Internet access through home computers remained very limited, Internet penetration in general reached about one-tenth of the population, partly due to the popularity of shared portals such as Internet cafés.

Government And Society

In 1947 the newly independent Pakistan consisted of two distinct parts: the smaller but more densely populated East Pakistan, centred on the Ganges-Brahmaputra delta region, and the much larger West Pakistan, occupying the northwestern portion of the Indian subcontinent. The country's government, functioning under a modified 1935 Government of India Act, was associated with a British-inherited parliamentary system, containing a strong central government as well as governments in the several provinces that also gave it a federal form. However, in 1971, after the country had experienced more than two decades of turbulent politics, the eastern region seceded and established itself as the independent state of Bangladesh. In the aftermath of that event, Pakistan (now reduced to the former West Pakistan) faced a number of political and economic problems and uncertainties about its future.

Several seemingly irreconcilable domestic conflicts have left their mark on the politics of Pakistan. The first of these occurred at the highest levels of leadership, involving the key political actors from the political parties, the higher bureaucracy, and the upper echelon of the armed forces (notably the Pakistani army). Constitutions in Pakistan have been less about limiting the power of authority and more a legal justification for arbitrary action. The country's several constitutions reflected more the preeminence of the person holding the highest office than the restrictions imposed on authority, and the national government consistently has been more personalized than institutionalized. The viceregalism of the colonial past has haunted Pakistan from its inception, and struggles for power are therefore more personal than constitutional. In addition, given the ever-present external threat posed by India, the military not only improved and modernized its fighting capability, but it also felt compelled to intervene in the country's political affairs when it perceived that civilian leadership was unable to govern. The result has been several military administrations (1958–69, 1969–71, 1977–88, and 1999–2008), which ruled Pakistan for roughly half of its history.

A second conflict has taken place between regional groups. The regions that originally made up Pakistan had to be fitted into a design not of their own choosing. The different cultural and historical circumstances, as well as natural and human endowments of those regions, have tested the unity of Pakistan time and again; the loss of East Pakistan demonstrated the failure of Pakistan's leaders to orchestrate a workable program of national integration. Even after that event, Pakistan has had difficulty reconciling rival claims. Punjab, being the largest and most significant province, has always been perceived as imposing its will on the others, and even attempts at establishing quotas for governmental and nongovernmental opportunities and resources have not satisfied the discontented. The demands for an independent Sindhu Desh for the Sindhis and a Pakhtunistan for the Pathans, and the violently rebellious circumstances in Balochistan in the 1980s and since 2002, illustrate the nature and depth of the problem of national integration. Because these various struggles have been directed against centralized authority, they have merged with the democratic struggle. But their express aims have been to secure greater regional representation in the bureaucratic and military establishment, especially in the higher echelons, and to achieve effective decentralization of powers within the federal system by emphasizing regional autonomy.

A third conflict sprang from the struggle over economic resources and development funds among the more-deprived regions and strata of the population. This resulted in a number of violent confrontations between the less-privileged segments of society and the state. Some of these confrontations, such as those in 1969 and 1977, led to the fall of constitutional government and the imposition of martial law.

A fourth conflict took place between the landed aristocracy that dominated Pakistan's political and economic life for much of the country's history and a new urban elite that began to assert itself in the late 1980s. One manifestation of this conflict was the struggle that broke out between Punjab provincial leaders and federal authorities in the late 1980s. Under the Islamic Democratic Alliance, the Punjab government continued to back the interests of the landed aristocracy, while the national government headed by Benazir Bhutto, with a more liberal bent and a wider base of support espoused the economic and social interests of urban groups and non-propertied classes. The two governments often clashed in the late 1980s, creating serious economic management problems. Issues regarding power sharing between the federal and provincial governments were largely ignored during the period of military rule in 1999–2008.

However, in the 21st century the success of any government in Pakistan civilian or military appeared to rest on the handling of what might be considered a fifth area of major conflict. Since 2001 the country has been confronted by a campaign of ceaseless terror, generally but not exclusively cast in religious terms, that has been mounted by religious forces opposed to secular modernism in all its forms. Government has always been mindful of the need to placate the religiously motivated populace, but finding a balance between those envisioning Pakistan as a theocratic state and those determined to pursue a liberal, progressive agenda has proved to be the most significant test. A climate of virtually irreconcilable forces has emerged, much of it manifested by external militant Islamic elements led by the al-Qaeda organization and a revived Afghan Taliban.

Constitutional framework

The task of framing a constitution was entrusted in 1947 to a Constituent Assembly that was also to function as the interim legislature under the 1935 Government of India Act, which was to be the interim constitution. Pakistan's first constitution was enacted by the Constituent Assembly in 1956. It followed the form of the 1935 act, allowing the president far-reaching powers to suspend federal and provincial parliamentary government (emphasizing the viceregal tradition of British India). It also included a "parity formula," by which representation in the National Assembly for East and West Pakistan would be decided on a parity, rather than population, basis. (A major factor in the political crisis of 1970–71 was abandonment of the parity formula and adoption of representation by population, giving East Pakistan an absolute majority in the National Assembly.)

In 1958 the constitution was abrogated, and martial law was instituted. A new constitution, promulgated in 1962, provided for the election of the president and national and provincial assemblies by something similar to an electoral college, composed of members of local councils. Although a federal form of government was retained, the assemblies had little power, which was, in effect, centralized through the authority of governors acting under the president. In April 1973 Pakistan's third constitution (since the 1935 act) was adopted by the National Assembly; it was suspended in 1977. In March 1981 a Provisional Constitutional Order was promulgated, providing a framework for government under martial law. Four years later a process was initiated for reinstating the constitution of 1973. By October 1985 a newly elected National Assembly had amended the constitution, giving extraordinary powers to the president, including the authority to appoint any member of the National Assembly as prime minister.

With the end of military rule in 1988 and following elections to the National Assembly held in November of that year, the new president used those powers to appoint a prime minister to form a civilian government under the amended 1973 constitution. In 1997 the prime minister pushed through two significant changes to the constitution. The first revoked the president's power to remove a sitting government, and the second gave the premier authority to dismiss from parliament any member not voting along party lines effectively eliminating the National Assembly's power to make a vote of no confidence. In 1999 a military government again came to power, and the constitution was suspended. The chief executive of that government initially ruled by decree and was made president in 2001. In 2002 the constitution was reinstated following a national referendum, though it included provisions (under the name Legal Framework order [LFO]) that restored presidential powers removed in 1997; most provisions of the LFO were formally incorporated into the constitution in 2003.

The amended constitution provides for a president as head of state and a prime minister as head of government; both must be Muslims. According to the constitution, the president is elected for a term of five years by the National Assembly, the Senate, and the four provincial assemblies. The prime minister is elected by the National Assembly. The president acts on the advice of the prime minister. Universal adult suffrage is practiced.

The National Assembly has 342 members, each of whom serves a five-year term. Of these, 272 seats are filled by direct popular election; 262

are for Muslim candidates, and 10 are for non-Muslims. Of the remaining seats, 60 are reserved for women, who are chosen by the major parties; in 2008 the assembly elected its first female speaker. The Senate has 100 members, each serving a six-year term. A portion of the senators are chosen by the provincial assemblies; others are appointed. One-third of the senators relinquish their seats every two years.

Local government

Pakistan's four provinces are divided into divisions, districts, and subdistricts (tehsils, or tahsils). These units are run by a hierarchy of administrators, such as the divisional commissioner, the deputy commissioner at the district level, and the subdivisional magistrate, subdivisional officer, or tehsildar (tahsildar) at the tehsil level. The key level is that of the district, where the deputy commissioner, although in charge of all branches of government, shares power with the elected chairman of the district council. During the period of British rule, the deputy commissioner was both the symbol and embodiment of the central government in remote locations. Expected to serve the constituents in numerous ways, the officer's responsibilities ranged from that of magistrate dispensing justice to record keeper, as well as provider of advice and guidance in managing the socioeconomic condition. Those multiple roles have varied little since independence, but increasing emphasis has been placed on self-help programs for the rural populace.

In addition to the provinces, Pakistan has the Federally Administered Tribal Areas (seven agencies along the Afghan border, adjacent to Khyber Pakhtunkhwa), which ostensibly are overseen by agents responsible to the federal government; the Islamabad Capital Territory; and a number of tribal areas that are administered by the provincial governments. The areas of Kashmir under Pakistani control are administered directly by the central government.

Justice

Under the constitution there is a formal division between the judiciary and the executive branches of government. The judiciary consists of the Supreme Court, the provincial high courts, and (under their jurisdiction and supervision) district courts that hear civil cases and sessions courts that hear criminal cases. There is also a magistracy that deals with cases brought by the police. The district magistrate (who, as deputy commissioner, also controls the police) hears appeals from magistrates under him; appeals may go from him to the sessions judge. The Supreme Court is a court of record. It has original, appellate, and advisory jurisdictions and is the highest court in the land. At the time of independence, Pakistan inherited legal codes and acts that have remained in force, subject to amendment. The independence of the judiciary has been tested at times, most notably in 2007, when Pres. Pervez Musharraf replaced the chief justice and several other Supreme Court justices who challenged his constitutional legitimacy. Pressure from lawyers' groups and opposition leaders led to the justices' reinstatement in 2009.

The judicial system also has a religious dimension; a reorientation to Islamic tenets and values was designed to make legal redress inexpensive and accessible to all persons. A complete code of Islamic laws was instituted, and the Federal Shariat Court, a court of Islamic law (Sharīʿah), was set up in the 1980s; the primary purpose of this court is to ascertain whether laws passed by parliament are congruent with the precepts of Islam. The Sharīʿah system operates alongside the more secular largely Anglo-Saxon system and legal tradition.

Political process

The role of Islam in the political and cultural unification of Pakistan has been controversial. Some factions have argued that Islamic ideology is the only cement that can bind together the country's culturally diverse peoples. Opposing factions have argued that the insistence on Islamic ideology, in opposition to regional demands expressed in secular and cultural idiom, has alienated regional groups and eroded national unity.

The Pakistan People's Party (PPP) was formed in 1968 by Zulfikar Ali Bhutto, working with a number of liberal leftists who wanted Pakistan to disregard the idiom of religion in politics in favour of a program of rapid modernization of the country and the introduction of a socialist economy. The PPP emerged as the majority party in West Pakistan in the elections of 1970 (though the Awami League in East Pakistan won the largest number of legislative seats). Following the disruption of the ensuing war, which produced the independent country of Bangladesh from East Pakistan, Bhutto was called to form a government in 1972. The PPP was suppressed under the military government of 1977–88 but returned to power in 1988–90 and 1993–96 under the leadership of Bhutto's daughter Benazir. In 2008, after the nine-year period of military rule, the party joined in a civilian coalition government.

The Muslim League, formed in 1906 in what is now Bangladesh, had spearheaded the Pakistan independence movement under Mohammed Ali Jinnah. However, by the time of the military coup in 1958 it had endured many setbacks and much fragmentation, and in 1962 it splintered into two parts, the Conventionist Pakistan Muslim League and the Council Muslim League. In the elections of 1970 it almost disappeared as a political party, but it was resurrected in 1985 and became the most important component of the Islamic Democratic Alliance, which took over Punjab's administration in 1988. Since then, Muslim League factions have been associated with powerful personalities (e.g., Nawaz Sharif and Pervez Musharraf).

The Islamic Assembly (Jamāʿat-e Islāmī), founded in 1941 by Abū al-Aʿlā Mawdūdī (Maududi), commands a great deal of support among the urban lower-middle classes (as well as having great influence abroad). Two other religious parties, the Assembly of Islamic Clergy (Jamīʿat ʿUlamāʾ-e Islām) and the Assembly of Pakistani Clergy (Jamīʿat ʿUlamāʾ-e Pakistan), have strong centres of support, the former in Karachi and the latter in the rural areas of the Khyber Pakhtunkhwa. Ethnic interests are served by organizations such as the Muttahida Qaumi Movement (formerly the Muhajir Qaumi Movement) in Karachi and Hyderabad, the Sindhi National Front in Sind, and the Balochistan Students Union in Balochistan.

Security

Pakistan's military has been led from inception by a highly trained and professional officer corps that has not hesitated, as a body, to involve itself in politics. The military consists of an army (the largest of the uniformed services), air force, and navy, as well as various paramilitary forces. Each of the services is headed by a chief of staff, and the chairman of Joint Chiefs of Staff is the senior officer of the military hierarchy.

The Pakistani military is one of the largest and best-trained in the world. Troops serve on a voluntary basis, and there is seldom a shortage of manpower. Military life in Pakistan is viewed as prestigious, and soldiers both active and retired can expect numerous perks and benefits from service. Enlisted personnel are given the chance to improve themselves through study and education, and officers are trained through the service academy or through several of the country's professional colleges.

The army is extremely well supplied, having devoted much of its considerable resources to the domestic production of weapons. The army has several thousand main battle tanks, armoured personnel carriers, and artillery pieces (both towed and self-propelled). The army also fields multiple-launch rocket systems and several short-range missile systems. The naval fleet consists of a variety of relatively small surface crafts (destroyers, frigates, missile craft, and patrol boats), as well as a small submarine fleet and an air arm. The air force flies several squadrons of high-performance fighter and ground-attack aircraft and a number of support and cargo planes.

Pakistan's military-industrial complex is large and well-funded. The country has developed its own main battle tanks and surface naval craft generally on designs contracted from foreign corporations and has fielded its own missile systems, several of which appear capable of delivering unconventional payloads. Pakistan announced its status as a country with nuclear weapons by detonating several devices in 1998. The nuclear-weapons program has always been the special preserve of the Pakistani army, although its scientists and technicians are drawn primarily from civilian life.

Internal security is provided by a variety of local and provincial police departments, as well as by paramilitary forces such as the Pakistan

Rangers, whose task is largely to provide border security. A number of paramilitary groups, such as the fabled Khyber Rifles, are officially part of the army but frequently engage in security work, such as combating terrorists. The Inter-Service Intelligence directorate is the country's largest intelligence collection body, and it has often been extremely successful in influencing government policy.

Health and welfare

Although Pakistan has made progress in improving health conditions, a large part of the population does not receive modern medical care. There are insufficient numbers of doctors and nurses, especially in rural areas. Sanitation facilities are also inadequate; only a small percentage of the population has access to safe drinking water and sanitary sewage disposal facilities. Malaria, tuberculosis and other respiratory diseases, and intestinal diseases are among the leading causes of death. Drug addiction is an increasingly serious problem; although drug use is reported most commonly among urban literate males, many others (for whom documentation is more difficult to compile) are also abusers.

Pakistan was among the first developing countries to establish a state-funded family planning program, which began in the early 1960s. The program ran into political difficulties in the late 1960s as a result of opposition by Islamic groups. The regimes of Zulfikar Ali Bhutto, Zia ul-Haq, and Benazir Bhutto gave family planning a relatively low priority.

Consequently, Pakistan's total fertility and population growth rates are relatively high by world standards this despite the fact that infant and maternal mortality rates are also relatively high.

The zakāt and ushr taxes are used to provide social welfare funds, which go to provincial, division, and district committees for distribution among organizations engaged in social welfare activities or directly to needy persons. Zakāt funds are also used for scholarships. The development of a number of nongovernmental organizations in the country and the increasing use of private religious endowments to assist the needy have been increasing. Those efforts have been most notable in the fields of education and basic health care.

Housing

Existing housing stocks do not meet national needs, and demands for housing have far outpaced the ability of the economy to produce more living space. Sufficient housing, in fact, has not traditionally been a high priority of the government, although in 1987 it did establish a National Housing Authority with the goal of developing housing units for the country's burgeoning low-income population. However, such attempts were abandoned in the 1990s for want of adequate resources. In 2001 a National Housing Policy was approved to review the status of nationwide housing and to identify sources of revenue, land availability, incentives to developers and contractors, and the conditions needed to make construction cost-effective.

There are three general classes of housing in Pakistan: pukka houses, built of substantial material such as stone, brick, cement, concrete, or timber; katchi (or kuchha ["ramshackle"]) houses, constructed of less-durable material (e.g., mud, bamboo, reeds, or thatch); and semi-pukka houses, which are a mix between the two. Housing stocks comprise an equal number of semi-pukka and katchi houses (about two-fifths each), and remaining houses (roughly one-fifth of the total) are the better-variety pukka houses. Urban areas are dominated by ramshackle neighbourhoods known locally as katchi abadis, which can be found in all cities. In such unplanned and unregulated areas, safe drinking water and proper sanitation are rare (as they are in rural areas), and the buildings themselves are often flimsy and unsafe. Throughout the country, roughly half of all urban residents live in such areas.

Pakistan's housing problem increased dramatically with the devastating 2005 earthquake in the northern areas, where more than half a million houses were destroyed or severely damaged over a vast area. The Pakistani government quickly established the Earthquake Reconstruction and Rehabilitation Authority (ERRA), which received funding from the World Bank and a large number of other sources. In addition to constructing new earthquake-resistant houses and reinforcing existing structures, the ERRA is repairing roads and other infrastructure in the region. Massive floods in 2010 destroyed or damaged an estimated 1.7 million houses, forcing millions of Pakistanis to move to temporary shelters.

Education

Pakistan's literacy rate is substantially lower than that of many developing countries; roughly half of all adults are literate, the literacy rate being significantly higher for males than for females. A substantial proportion of those who are literate, however, have not had any formal education. Educational levels for women are much lower than those for men. The share of females in educational levels progressively diminishes above the primary school level.

Education in Pakistan is not compulsory. Since independence Pakistan has increased the number of primary and secondary schools, and the number of students enrolled has risen dramatically. Teacher training has been promoted by the government and by international agencies. Higher education is available at vocational schools, technical schools, and colleges throughout the country. The oldest university is the University of the Punjab (established 1882), and the largest institutions are Allama Iqbal Open University (1974), in Islamabad, the University of Peshawar (1950), and the University of Karachi (1950). Other universities established during the 20th century include Quaid-i-Azam University (1967; called the University of Islamabad until 1976), the Khyber Pakhtunkhwa Agricultural University in Peshawar (1981), the International Islamic University in Islamabad (1980), the Aga Khan University in Karachi (1983), and the Lahore University for Management Sciences (1986). Most university classes are taught in Urdu or English.

Education suffered a major setback in the 1970s as a result of the nationalization of private schools and colleges. The reversal of that policy in the 1980s led to a proliferation of private institutions, particularly in the large cities. In the 1980s the government also began to focus on the Islamization of the curriculum and the increased use of Urdu as the medium of instruction. During that period there was also an increase in the number of madrassas (Islamic schools) established throughout the country, particularly in poorer areas. (The added incentive of such institutions has been that most are residential schools, providing room and board at no cost in addition to a free education.) Although many of these schools provide good quality education in religious as well as secular subjects, others are simply maktabs (primary schools) that provide no basic education, even for older students, beyond the memorization of scripture; a number of those particularly schools found along the Afghan border have been recruiting and training centres for jihadist groups.

The more-Westernized segments of the population prefer to send their children to private schools, which continue to offer Western-style education and instruction in English. A number of private schools offer college entrance examinations administered by educational agencies in the United States and the United Kingdom, and many graduates of these schools are educated abroad. The division of the educational system into a private Westernized section and a state-run Islamized section has thus caused social tensions and exacerbated the problem of "brain drain," the emigration to the West of many of the better-educated members of the population.

Cultural Life

Pakistan shares influences that have shaped the cultures of South Asia. There are thus wider regional similarities extending beyond the national boundaries; cultural ways in Pakistan are broadly similar to those experienced in large parts of Afghanistan and northern India. This entire region was deeply influenced by the Arabic-Persian culture that arrived with Muslim conquerors beginning roughly a millennium ago. On the other hand, the specific regional cultures of Pakistan present a picture of rich diversity, making it difficult to speak of a single Pakistani culture. Residents of Khyber Pakhtunkhwa, for example, lead lives similar to fellow Pashtuns in Afghanistan. In other parts of the country, Urdu-speaking muhajirs brought with them many cultural ways and values found among the Hindu, Sikh, and Muslim populations of northern India.

Daily life and social customs

Throughout Pakistan, as in most agrarian societies, family organization is strongly patriarchal, and most people live with large extended families, often in the same house or family compound. The eldest male, whether he is the father, grandfather, or paternal uncle, is the family leader and makes all significant decisions regarding the family and its members. Traditionally, a woman's place in society has been secondary to that of men, and she has been restricted to the performance of domestic chores and to fulfilling the role of a dutiful wife and mother. However, in the Punjab, cotton picking is exclusively a woman's job, and women may keep the money thus earned for their own purposes.

In wealthy peasant and landowner households and in urban middle-class families, the practice of keeping women in seclusion (purdah) is still common; when women leave their houses, they typically cover their heads. Among the rural poor, women have duties on the farm as well as in the house and do not customarily observe purdah. Houses of those who practice purdah have a men's section (mardānah) at the front of the house, so that visitors do not disturb the women, who are secluded in the women's section (zanānah) in the rear. Women's subordinate status in Pakistan also is evident in the practice of "honour killings," in which a woman may be killed by a male relative if she is thought to have brought dishonour on the family or clan.

Among the wealthiest Pakistanis, Western education and modes of living have eliminated purdah, but, in general, even among that group, attitudes toward women in society and the family often have been viewed by outsiders as antiquated. Change has occurred most rapidly among the urban middle-income group, inspired by increasing access to the West as well as by the entry of women into the workforce and into government service. An increasing number of middle-class women have stopped observing purdah, and the education of women has been encouraged. Some women have gained distinction in the professions; some of Pakistan's leading politicians, journalists, and teachers have been women, and a woman has served as prime minister and as speaker of parliament.

In traditional parts of Pakistan, social organization revolves around kinship rather than around the caste system that is used in India. The baradari (berādarī; patrilineage, literally "brotherhood") is the most important social institution. Endogamy is widely practiced, often to a degree that would be considered inappropriate in Western society; the preferred marriage for a man within many Pakistani communities is with his father's brother's daughter, and among many other groups marriages are invariably within the baradari. The lineage elders constitute a council that adjudicates disputes within the lineage and acts on behalf of the lineage with the outside world for example, in determining political allegiances. In contemporary Pakistan, the question of class distinction based on historic patterns of social interaction has become blurred by the tendency to pretend that one has lineage to a nobler ancestor. However, irrespective of the questionable authenticity of a claim to a particular title, the classification of social status persists.

Pakistani clothing styles are similar in many ways to those found in India. The shalwar-kamiz combination a long knee-length shirt (kamiz, camise) over loose-fitting pants (shalwar) is the most common traditional form of attire. As a more formal overgarment, men wear a knee-length coat known as a sherwani; women frequently wear a light shawl called a dupatta. Among conservative Muslim communities, women sometimes wear the burqa, a full-length garment that may or may not cover the face. In earlier generations, the fez hat was popular among Muslim men, but more often the woolen, boat-shaped Karakul hat (popularized by Mohammed Ali Jinnah) is associated with Pakistan; however, many other hat styles are worn, especially in tribal areas. Western clothes are popular among the urban young, and combinations of Western and Pakistani styles can be seen in the streets.

Pakistani cuisine also has affinities with that of India. Curry dishes are common, as are a variety of vegetables, including potatoes, eggplant, and okra. Each region (and, often, each household) has its own preferred mixture of spices the term masala is used to describe such a mixture. In addition to the many spices that are also associated with other countries of South Asia, yogurt is a common ingredient. Favourite meats include chicken, mutton, and lamb. Lentils are a standard dish, and various types of wheat bread are the national staple. The most common breads are chapati (unleavened flat bread) and naan (slightly leavened). Pakistanis drink a great deal of hot tea (chai), and lassi (a type of yogurt drink), sherbet, and lemonade are popular. As in most Muslim countries, alcoholic beverages are considered culturally inappropriate, but there are several domestic breweries and distilleries.

Muslim Pakistanis celebrate the two major Islamic holidays, ʿĪd al-Fiṭr (which marks the end of Ramadan) and ʿĪd al-Aḍḥā (which marks the end of the hajj), as well as the Prophet Muhammad's birthday (the religious holidays are based on a lunar calendar and vary from year to year). Mohammed Ali Jinnah's birthday (December 25) is a celebrated holiday. Independence Day is August 14, and Pakistan Day is March 23 (celebrating the Lahore [Pakistan] Resolution of 1940). There are a number of other major and minor holidays.

The arts

Pakistan's cultural heritage dates to more than 5,000 years ago, to the period of the Indus civilization. However, the emphasis on Islamic ideology has brought about a strong romantic identification with Islamic culture not only that of the Indian subcontinent but of the broader Islamic world. Literature, notably poetry, is the richest of all Pakistani art forms; music and, especially, modern dance have received less attention. The visual arts too play little part in popular folk culture. Painting and sculpture, however, have made considerable progress as expressions of an increasingly sophisticated urban culture.

Pakistan shares with the other parts of South Asia the great Mughal heritage in art, literature, architecture, and manners. The ruins of Mohenjo-daro, the ancient city of Taxila, and the Rohtas Fort of Shīr Shah of Sūr are but a few of the places in Pakistan that have been named UNESCO World Heritage sites. The Mosque of the Pearls, Badshahi Mosque, and Shalimar Garden, all in Lahore, are among the country's architectural gems.

Popular traditional folk dances include the bhangra (an explosive dance developed in Punjab) and khatak steps. The khatak is a martial dance of the tribal Pashtuns that involves energetic miming of warriors' exploits. There are a number of traditional dances associated with women; these include a humorous song and dance called the giddha, a whirling dance performed by girls and young women called the kikli, and a form in which dancers snap their fingers and clap their hands while bounding in a circle. The luddi is a Punjabi dance usually performed by males, typically to celebrate a victory formerly victory in a military conflict but now in a sports contest.

Music has long been a part of Pakistani culture, and the country was greatly influenced by the northern Indian tradition of Hindustani music. Traditional and local styles abound. The ghazal, a type of romantic poem, is often put to music. Ghazal singers such as Mehdi Hassan and Ghulam Ali have developed a broad following at home and abroad. Qawwali, a form of devotional singing associated with Sufism, is also widely practiced and has influenced a number of popular styles. One of its greatest adherents, Nusrat Fateh Ali Khan, became famous in Pakistan and the broader world. Traditional instruments include the sitar, rabab (a fiddlelike stringed instrument), and dhol (bass drum).

Western-style popular music has been slow to develop in Pakistan, although by the early 21st century there were a number of singers, both men and women, who were considered to be pop stars. Among these were the sibling duo Nazia Hassan and Zoheb Hassan, the crooner Alamgir, and the rock bands Vital Signs and Junoon, a group whose music was inspired by Sufism.

Poetry is a popular rather than an esoteric art, and public poetry recitations, called mushāʻirahs, are organized like musical concerts. Sir Muhammad Iqbal, one of the major forces behind the establishment of Pakistan (though he died a decade before the country's founding), was a noted poet in Persian and Urdu. Pashto, Urdu, and Sindhi poets are regional and national heroes.

Traditional Punjabi theatre was generally a venue for lower-class street performers and tended to be of a comic, slapstick variety. Commercial theatre in northern India and Pakistan, however, did not appear until the mid-19th century, and then largely in the Urdu language and among the Parsi community. After partition most professional actors, directors, and writers in the Muslim community gravitated toward the theatre and cinema of India (one important exception being the renowned actress and singer Noor Jehan). The cinema is the most popular form of entertainment in Pakistan. Many feature films are produced each year, mostly in the Punjabi and Urdu languages, and Pakistanis have developed a devotion to movies produced in India despite the political differences between the two countries. Other noted film stars are Sultan Rahi (Sultan Muhammad) and Mohammad Ali and his wife, Zeba. The songs and music used in Pakistani films have a distinctive character and are often reproduced on records or digital discs and broadcast on the radio.

Cultural institutions

Pakistan's long and rich history is reflected in the number of fine museums found there. The Lahore Museum (1894) has a splendid collection of arts and crafts, jewelry, and sculpture from various historical periods. The National Museum of Pakistan, in Karachi (1950), has a number of galleries, which include displays of objects from the Indus civilization and examples of Gandhara art. There are a number of archaeological museums and several private museums with specialized exhibits. The Taxila Institute of Asian Civilizations (founded 1997) was merged administratively with Quaid-i-Azam University in Islamabad in 2007. The National College of Arts (founded in 1872 as the Mayo School of Industrial Art) in Lahore is the only degree-granting institute of fine arts in the country. There are several private art galleries located in larger cities.

Sports and recreation

Cricket is a national favourite, and the country has produced some of the world's best players, including Asif Iqbal and Imran Khan. The Pakistani national team won the World Cup in 1992 and has a number of victories in one-day international competitions. Cricket is governed by the Pakistan Cricket Board.

Among team sports, only field hockey compares to cricket in popularity. The country has won World Cup and Olympic championships in field hockey several times. Squash is one of the most popular individual sports; Pakistan dominated world competition during the 1980s and '90s, when Jahangir Khan and Jansher Khan (who are not related) won a combined 14 World Open Championships.

Pakistan has competed in the Olympic Summer Games since 1948 (though the country boycotted the 1980 Moscow Games following the Soviet invasion of Afghanistan). It has not been represented at the

Winter Games. Almost all the country's success has been in field hockey, including gold medal wins in 1960, 1968, and 1984.

Media and publishing

Government-owned radio and television traditionally have been used in an attempt to harness folk cultural traditions (especially in song, music, and drama) for political and nonpolitical purposes. In 2002 the Pakistan Electronic Media Regulatory Authority (PEMRA) was established to regulate and license privately owned radio, television, and satellite broadcasting facilities. Censorship, particularly of newspapers, is widespread, but Pakistanis have access to a variety of information media via satellite television (ownership of dishes is growing rapidly) and the Internet as well as newspapers and journals. Newspapers, in particular those published in Urdu, Sindhi, and English, have a wide readership, and many are available in both print and online versions. Pakistan has numerous publishing houses, which print books mostly in English and Urdu.

History

This section presents the history of Pakistan from the partition of British India (1947) to the present. For a discussion of the earlier history of the region, see India.

Background to partition

The call for establishing an independent Islamic state on the Indian subcontinent can be traced to a 1930 speech by Sir Muhammad Iqbal, a poet-philosopher and, at the time, president of the All India Muslim League (after Pakistan's independence, shortened to Muslim League). It was his argument that the four northwestern provinces and regions of British India i.e., Sind (Sindh), Balochistan, Punjab, and North-West Frontier Province (now Khyber Pakhtunkhwa) should one day be joined to become a free and independent Muslim state. The limited character of this proposal can be judged from its geographic rather than demographic dimensions. Iqbal's Pakistan included only those Muslims residing in the Muslim-majority areas in the northwestern quadrant of the subcontinent. It ignored the millions of other Muslims living throughout the subcontinent, and it certainly did not take into account the Muslim majority of Bengal in the east. Moreover, Iqbal's vision did not reflect the interests of others outside the Muslim League seeking liberation from colonial rule, and it did not conform to ideas reflected in Islamic expressions that spoke of a single Muslim community (ummah) or people (qawm), explaining in no small way why many other Muslim leaders e.g., Abul Kalam Azad, Abdul Ghaffar Khan, and, later, Khizar Hayat Khan Tiwana were less than enthused with his proposal.

Also missing at the time was a name to describe such a South Asian country where Muslims would be masters of their own destiny. That task fell to Choudhary Rahmat Ali, a young Muslim student studying at Cambridge in England, who best captured the poet-politician's yearnings in the single word Pakistan. In a 1933 pamphlet, Now or Never, Rahmat Ali and three Cambridge colleagues coined the name as an acronym for Punjab, Afghania (North-West Frontier Province), Kashmir, and Indus-Sind, combined with the -stan suffix from Baluchistan (Balochistan). It was later pointed out that, when translated from Urdu, Pakistan could also mean "Land of the Pure."

The Muslim League and Mohammed Ali Jinnah

Long before the British invaded and seized control of the subcontinent, Muslim armies had conquered the settled populations in the rolling flat land that stretched from the foothills of the Hindu Kush to the city of Delhi and the Indo-Gangetic Plain and eastward to Bengal. The last and most successful of the Muslim conquerors was the Mughal dynasty (1526–1857), which eventually spread its authority over virtually the entire subcontinent. British superiority coincided with Mughal decline, and, following a period of European successes and Mughal failures on the battlefield, the British brought an end to Mughal power. The last Mughal emperor was exiled following the failed Indian Mutiny of 1857–58.

Less than three decades after that revolt, the Indian National Congress was formed to give political representation to British India's indigenous people. Although membership in the Congress was open to all, Hindu participants overwhelmed the Muslim members. The All India Muslim League, organized in 1906, aimed to give Muslims a voice so as to counter what was then perceived as the growing influence of the Hindus under British rule. Mohammed Ali Jinnah, earlier a prominent Muslim member of the Congress, assumed leadership of the league following his break with Congress leader Mohandas K. Gandhi. A firm believer in the Anglo-Saxon rule of law and a close associate of Iqbal, Jinnah questioned the security of the Muslim minority in an India dominated by essentially Hindu authority. Declaring Islam was endangered by a revived Hindu assertiveness, Jinnah and the league posited a "two-nation theory" that argued Indian Muslims were entitled to and therefore required a separate, self-governing state in a reconstituted subcontinent.

The British intention to grant self-government to India along the lines of British parliamentary democracy is evident in the Government of India Act of 1935. Up to that time, the question of Hindus and Muslims sharing in the governance of India was generally acceptable, although it was also acknowledged that Hindus more so than Muslims had accommodated themselves to British customs and the colonial manner of administration. Moreover, following the failed Indian Mutiny, Hindus were more eager to adopt British behaviours and ideas, whereas Indian Muslims bore the brunt of British wrath. The Mughal Empire was formally dissolved in 1858, and its last ruler was banished from the subcontinent. Believing they had been singled out for punishment, India's Muslim population was reluctant to adopt British ways or take advantage of English educational opportunities. As a consequence of these different positions, Hindus advanced under British rule at the expense of their Muslim counterparts, and when Britain opened the civil service to the native population, the Hindus virtually monopolized the postings. Although influential Muslims such as Sayyid Ahmad Khan recognized the growing power imbalance and encouraged Muslims to seek European education and entry into the colonial civil service, they also realized that catching up to the more progressive and advantaged Hindus was an impossible task.

It was this juxtaposition of an emerging feeling of Hindu superiority and a sustained sense among Muslims of inferiority that the All India Muslim League addressed in its claim to represent the Muslims of India. Unlike other Muslim movements of the period, the Muslim League articulated the sentiments of the attentive and at the same time more moderate elements among India's Muslim population. The Muslim League, with Jinnah as its spokesman, was also the preferred organization from the standpoint of British authority. Unlike Gandhi's practices of civil disobedience, the lawyer Jinnah (who was called to the bar at Lincoln's Inn, London) was more inclined to promote the rule of law in seeking separation from imperial rule. Jinnah, therefore, was more open to a negotiated settlement, and, indeed, his first instinct was to preserve the unity of India, albeit with adequate safeguards for the Muslim community. For Jinnah, the Lahore (later Pakistan) Resolution of 1940, which called for an independent Muslim state or states in India, did not at first imply the breakup of the Indian union.

World War II (1939–45) proved to be the catalyst for an unanticipated change in political power. Under pressure from a variety of popular national movements notably those organized by the Congress and led by Gandhi, the war-weakened British were forced to consider abandoning India. In response to the Congress campaign that Britain quit India, London sent a mission headed by Sir Richard Stafford Cripps (the Cripps Mission) to New Delhi in early 1942 with the promise that Congress's cooperation in the war effort would be rewarded with greater self-rule and possibly even independence when the war ended. Gandhi and the other Congress leaders, however, could not be appeased, and their insistence that Britain allow for a transfer of power while the war raged produced an impasse and the failure of the mission.

During that period, the Jinnah-led Muslim League was substantially less aggressive in seeking immediate British withdrawal. The differences between the two groups were not lost on Britain, and the eventual defeat of Germany and Japan set the scene for the drama that resulted in the partition of British India and the independence of

Pakistan. The new postwar Labour Party government of Clement Attlee, succeeding the Conservative Winston Churchill government, was determined to terminate its authority in India. A cabinet mission led by William Pethick-Lawrence was sent in 1946 to discuss and possibly arrange the mechanisms for the transfer of power to indigenous hands. Throughout the deliberations the British had to contend with two prominent players: Gandhi and the Congress and Jinnah and the Muslim League. Jinnah laboured to find a suitable formula that addressed the mutual and different needs of the subcontinent's two major communities. When Pethick-Lawrence's mission proved unequal to the task of reconciling the parties, the last chance for a compromise solution was lost. Each of the major actors blamed the other for the breakdown in negotiations, with Jinnah insisting on the realization of the "two-nation theory." The goal now was nothing less than the creation of a sovereign, independent Pakistan.

Birth of the new state

Like India, Pakistan achieved independence as a dominion within the Commonwealth in August 1947. However, the leaders of the Muslim League rejected Lord Mountbatten, the last British viceroy of India, to be Pakistan's first governor-general, or head of state in contrast to the Congress, which made him India's chief executive. Wary of Britain's machinations and desirous of rewarding Jinnah their "Great Leader"

(Quaid-e Azam), a title he was given before independence, Pakistanis made him their governor-general; his lieutenant in the party, Liaquat Ali Khan, was named prime minister. Pakistan's first government, however, had a difficult task before it. Unlike Muhammad Iqbal's earlier vision for Pakistan, the country had been formed from the two regions where Muslims were the majority; the northwestern portion he had espoused and the territories; and the eastern region of Bengal province (which itself had also been divided between India and Pakistan). Pakistan's two wings, therefore, were separated by some 1,000 miles (1,600 km) of sovereign Indian territory with no simple routes of communication between them. Further complicating the work of the new Pakistani government was the realization that the wealth and resources of British India had been granted to India. Pakistan had little but raw enthusiasm to sustain it, especially during those months immediately following partition. In fact, Pakistan's survival seemed to hang in the balance. Of all the well-organized provinces of British India, only the comparatively backward areas of Sind, Balochistan, and the North-West Frontier Province came to Pakistan intact. The otherwise more developed provinces of Punjab and Bengal were divided, and, in the case of Bengal, Pakistan received little more than the densely populated rural hinterland.

Adding to the dilemma of the new and untested Pakistan government was the crisis in Kashmir, which provoked a war between the two neighbouring states in the period immediately following their independence. Both Pakistan and India intended to make Kashmir a component of their respective unions, and the former princely state quickly became disputed territory with India and Pakistan controlling portions of it and a flash point for future conflicts. Economically, the situation in Pakistan was desperate; materials from the Indian factories were cut off from Pakistan, disrupting the new country's meagre industry, commerce, and agriculture. Moreover, the character of the partition and its aftermath had caused the flight of millions of refugees on both sides of the divide, accompanied by terrible massacres. The exodus of such a vast number of desperate people in each direction required an urgent response, which neither country was prepared to manage, least of all Pakistan.

As a consequence of the unresolved war in Kashmir and the communal bloodletting in the streets of both countries, India and Pakistan each came to see the other as its mortal enemy. The Pakistanis had anticipated a division of India's material, financial, and military assets. In fact, there would be none. New Delhi displayed no intention of dividing the assets of British India with its major adversary, thereby establishing a balance between the two countries. Moreover, India's superior geopolitical position and, most importantly, its control of the vital rivers that flowed into Pakistan meant that the Muslim country's water supplies were at the mercy of its larger, hostile neighbour.

Pakistan's condition was so precarious following independence that many observers believed the country could hardly survive six months and that India's goal of a unified subcontinent remained a distinct possibility.

The early republic

Mohammed Ali Jinnah died in September 1948, only 13 months after Pakistan's independence. Nevertheless, it was Jinnah's dynamic personality that sustained the country during those difficult months. Assuming responsibility as the nation's chief and virtually only decision maker, Jinnah held more than the ceremonial position of his British counterpart in India. But there too lay a special problem. Jinnah's formidable presence, even though weakened by illness, loomed large over the polity, and the other members of government were totally subordinate to his wishes. Thus, although Pakistan commenced its independent existence as a democratic entity with a parliamentary system, the representative aspects of the political system were muted by the role of the Quaid-e Azam. In effect, Jinnah, not India's Mountbatten, perpetuated the viceregal tradition that had been central to Britain's colonial rule. Unlike India, where Gandhi opted to remain outside government and where India's prime minister, Jawaharlal Nehru, and the parliament administered to the country, in Pakistan the parliament and members of the governing cabinet were cast in a subordinate role.

Liaquat Ali Khan

When Jinnah died, a power vacuum was created that his successors in the Muslim League had great difficulty filling. Khwaja Nazimuddin, the chief minister of East Bengal, was called on to take up the office of governor-general. Known for his mild manner, it was assumed Nazimuddin would not interfere with the parliamentary process and would permit the prime minister to govern the country. Prime Minister Liaquat Ali Khan, however, lacked the necessary constituency in the regions that formed Pakistan. Nor did he possess Jinnah's strength of personality. Liaquat therefore was hard put to cope with entrenched and vested interests, particularly in regions where local leaders dominated. Jinnah had worked hard to mollify competing and ambitious provincial leaders, and Liaquat, himself a refugee (muhajir) from India, simply did not have the stature to pick up where Jinnah had left off.

Liaquat was eager to give the country a new constitution, but such an undertaking was delayed by controversy, particularly over the distribution of provincial powers and over representation. Although what had been East Bengal (and became East Pakistan) contained the majority of Pakistan's population, the Punjab nevertheless judged itself the more significant of the Pakistani provinces. The Punjabis had argued that East Bengal was populated by a significant number of Hindus whose loyalty to the Muslim country was questionable. Any attempt therefore to provide East Bengal with representation commensurate to its population would be challenged by the Punjab. Although Jinnah had voiced the view that Muslims, Hindus, Christians, and all religious denominations were equal citizens in the new Pakistani state, Liaquat could not neutralize this controversy, nor could he resolve the issue of provincial representation. Forced to sell his vision to the people of Pakistan directly, Liaquat engaged in a number of public speaking engagements, and it was at such a meeting, in Rawalpindi in October 1951, that he was killed by an assassin's bullet.

Political decline and bureaucratic ascendancy

Nazimuddin assumed the premiership on Liaquat's death, and Ghulam Muhammad took his place as the governor-general. Ghulam Muhammad, a Punjabi, had been Jinnah's choice to serve as Pakistan's first finance minister and was an old and successful civil servant. The juxtaposition of these two very different personalities Nazimuddin, known for his piety and reserved nature, and Ghulam Muhammad, a staunch advocate of strong, efficient administration was hardly fortuitous. Nazimuddin's assumption of the office of prime minister meant the country would have a weak head of government, and, with Ghulam Muhammad as governor-general, a strong head of state. Pakistan's viceregal tradition was again in play.

In 1953 riots erupted in the Punjab, supposedly over a demand by militant Muslim groups that the Aḥmadiyyah sect be declared non-Muslim and that all members of the sect holding public office be dismissed. (Special attention was directed at Sir Muhammad Zafrulla Khan, an Aḥmadiyyah and Pakistan's first foreign minister.) Nazimuddin was held responsible for the disorder, especially for his inability to quell it, and Ghulam Muhammad took the opportunity to dismiss the prime minister and his government. Although another Bengali, Muhammad Ali Bogra, replaced Nazimuddin, there was no ignoring the fact that the viceregal tradition was continuing to dominate Pakistani political life and that Ghulam Muhammad, a bureaucrat and never truly a politician, with others like him, controlled Pakistan's destiny.

Meanwhile, in East Bengal (East Pakistan), considerable opposition had developed against the Muslim League, which had managed the province since independence. This tension was capped in 1952 by a series of riots that sprang from a Muslim League attempt to make Urdu the only national language of Pakistan, although Bengali the predominant language of the eastern sector was spoken by a larger proportion of Pakistan's population. The language riots galvanized the Bengalis, and they rallied behind their more indigenous parties to thwart what they argued was an effort by the West Pakistanis, notably the Punjabis, to transform East Bengal into a distant "colony."

With a Punjabi bureaucratic elite in firm control of the central government, in March 1954 the last in a series of provincial elections was held in East Bengal. The contest was between the Muslim League government and a "United Front" of parties led by the Krishak Sramik party of Fazlul Haq (Fazl ul-Haq) and the Awami League of Hussein Shaheed Suhrawardy, Mujibur Rahman, and Maulana Bhashani. When the ballots were counted, the Muslim League had not only lost the election, it had been virtually eliminated as a viable political force in the province. Fazlul Haq was given the opportunity to form the new provincial government in East Bengal, but, before he could convene his cabinet, riots erupted in the factories south of the East Bengali capital of Dhaka (Dacca). This instability provided the central government with the opportunity to establish "governor's rule" in the province and overturn the United Front's electoral victory. Iskander Mirza, a civil servant, former defense secretary, and minister in the central government, was sent to rule over the province until such time as stability could be assured.

Iskander Mirza had no intention of implementing the results of the election, nor did he wish to install a new Muslim League government in East Bengal. But the Muslim League's defeat and de facto elimination in the province necessitated realigning the Constituent Assembly still grappling with the drafting of a national constitution at the centre. Before this could be done, however, the Constituent

Assembly moved to curtail Ghulam Muhammad's viceregal powers. The governor-general's response to this parliamentary effort to undermine his authority was to dissolve that body and reorganize the central government. The country's high court cited the extraordinary powers of the chief executive and ruled not to reverse his action. The court, however, insisted that another constituent assembly should be organized and that constitution making should not be interrupted. Ghulam Muhammad assembled a "cabinet of talents" that included major personalities such as Iskander Mirza, Gen. Mohammad Ayub Khan (the army chief of staff), and H.S. Suhrawardy (the last chief minister of undivided Bengal, and the only Bengali with national credentials).

In 1955 the bureaucrats who now took control of what remained of the Muslim League combined the four provinces of West Pakistan into one administrative unit and argued for parity in any future national parliament between West Pakistan and East Bengal (now officially renamed East Pakistan). Ghulam Muhammad, by then seriously ill, was forced to relinquish his office, and Iskander Mirza succeeded to the post of governor-general. In the meantime a new Constituent Assembly was seated; and in 1956 that body, under new leadership but still subject to the power of the bureaucracy, and now to the military as well, completed Pakistan's long-awaited constitution, using the parity formula that supposedly gave equal power to both wings of the country.

The constitution of 1956 embodied objectives regarding religion and politics that had been set out in the Basic Principles Report published in 1950, one of which was to declare the country an Islamic republic. The national parliament was to comprise one house of 300 members, equally representing East and West Pakistan. Ten additional seats were reserved for women, again with half coming from each region. The prime minister and cabinet were to govern according to the will of the parliament, with the president exercising only reserve powers. Pakistan's first president was its last governor-general, Iskander Mirza, but at no time did he consider bowing to the wishes of the parliament.

Along with a close associate, Dr. Khan Sahib, a former premier of the North-West Frontier Province, Mirza formed the Republican Party and made Khan Sahib the chief minister of the new province of West Pakistan. The Republican Party was assembled to represent the landed interests in West Pakistan, the basic source of all political power. Never an organized body, the Republican Party lacked an ideology or a platform and merely served the feudal interests in West Pakistan.

Mirza made an alliance between the Republican Party and the East Pakistan Awami League and called on H.S. Suhrawardy to assume the office of prime minister. But the quixotic character of the alliance between the two parties, as well as the distance between the major personalities, produced only a short-lived association. Suhrawardy suffered the same fate as his predecessors and was ousted from office by Mirza without a vote of confidence. Unable to sustain alliances or govern in accordance with the constitution, the central government mirrored the chaos in the provinces. This was especially true in East Pakistan, where even in the absence of the Muslim League, the different provincial parties now further complicated by the formation of the National Awami Party, in 1957 struggled against forces that could not be reconciled. Pakistan was close to becoming unmanageable. The situation had become so grave that Khan Sahib circulated his idea that it was time to cease the political charade and give all power to a dictator.

Military government

In light of such dissent and with secession being voiced in different regions of the country (notably in East Pakistan and the North-West Frontier Province), on Oct. 7, 1958, Mirza proclaimed the 1956 constitution abrogated, closed the national and provincial assemblies, and banned all political party activity. He declared that the country was under martial law and that Gen. Mohammad Ayub Khan had been made chief martial-law administrator. Mirza claimed that it was his intention to lift martial law as soon as possible and that a new constitution would be drafted; and on October 27 he swore in a new cabinet, naming Ayub Khan prime minister, while three lieutenant generals were given ministerial posts. The eight civilian members in the cabinet included businessmen and lawyers, one being a young newcomer, Zulfikar Ali Bhutto, a powerful landlord from Sind province. However, Ayub Khan viewed his being named prime minister as the president's attempt to end his military career and ultimately to force him into oblivion. Clearly, the country could not afford two paramount rulers at the same time. Therefore, if one had to go, Ayub Khan decided that it should be Mirza. On the evening of October 27, Ayub Khan's senior generals presented Mirza with an ultimatum of facing permanent exile or prosecution by a military tribunal. Mirza immediately left for London, never again to return to Pakistan. Soon thereafter, Ayub Khan, who now assumed the rank of field marshal, proclaimed his assumption of the presidency.

Martial law lasted 44 months. During that time, a number of army officers took over vital civil service posts. Many politicians were excluded from public life under an Electoral Bodies (Disqualification) Order; a similar purge took place among civil servants. Yet, Ayub Khan argued that Pakistan was not yet ready for a full-blown experiment in parliamentary democracy and that the country required a period of tutelage and honest government before a new constitutional system could be established. He therefore initiated a plan for "basic democracies," consisting of rural and urban councils directly elected by the people that would be concerned with local governance and would assist in programs of grassroots development. Elections took place in January 1960, and the Basic Democrats, as they became known, were at once asked to endorse and thus legitimate Ayub Khan's presidency. Of the 80,000 Basic Democrats, 75,283 affirmed their support. Basic democracies was a tiered system inextricably linked to the bureaucracy, and the Basic Democrats occupied the lowest rung of a ladder that was connected to the country's administrative subdistricts (tehsils, or tahsils), districts, and divisions.

It was soon clear that the real power in the system resided in the bureaucrats who had dominated decision making since colonial times. Nevertheless, the basic democracies system was linked to a public-works program that was sponsored by the United States. The combined effort was meant to confer responsibility for village and municipal development to the local population. Self-reliance was the watchword of the overall program, and Ayub Khan and his advisers, as well as important donor countries, believed the arrangement would provide material benefits and possibly even expose people to self-governing experiences.

Ayub Khan also established a constitutional commission to advise on a form of government more appropriate to the country's political culture, and his regime introduced a number of reforms. Not the least of these was the Muslim Family Laws Ordinance of 1961, which restricted polygamy and provided more rights and protection for women. He also authorized the development of family-planning programs that were aimed at tackling the dilemma of Pakistan's growing population. Such actions angered the more conservative and religiously disposed members of society, who also swelled the ranks of the opposition. Under pressure to make amends and to placate the guardians of Islamic tradition, the family-planning program was eventually scrapped.

An important feature of the Ayub Khan regime was the quickening pace of economic growth. During the initial phase of independence, the annual growth rate was less than 3 percent, and that was scarcely ahead of the rate of population growth. Just prior to the military coup, the rate of growth was even smaller. During the Ayub Khan era with assistance from external sources, notably the United States the country accelerated economic growth, and by 1965 it had advanced to more than 6 percent per annum. Development was particularly vigorous in the manufacturing sector, but considerable attention was also given to agriculture. U.S. assistance was especially prominent in combating water logging and salinity problems that resulted from irrigation in the more vital growing zones. Moreover, plans were implemented that launched the "green revolution" in Pakistan, and new hybrid wheat and rice varieties were introduced with the goal of increasing yields.

Despite positive economic developments, overall, most investment was directed toward West Pakistan, and the divisions between East and West grew during this period. Ayub Khan attempted to answer Bengali fears of becoming second-class citizens when after work was begun, at his order, on building a new Pakistan capital at Islamabad he declared it was his intention to build a second, or legislative, capital near Dhaka, in East Pakistan. However, the start of construction on the new second capital did not placate the Bengalis, who were angered by Ayub Khan's abrogation of the 1956 constitution, his failure to hold national elections, and the decision to sustain martial law.

East Pakistanis had many grievances, and in no instance did they genuinely believe their purposes and concerns could be served under Ayub Khan's military government. Subsequent developments only served to enforce these beliefs. Water rights agreements signed with India and hydroelectric projects along the Indus River benefited the West, as did military agreements reached with the United States. The Pakistani officer class was largely from West Pakistan, and all the key army and air installations were located there even in the case of naval capability, Karachi was a far more formidable base of operations than Chittagong in East Pakistan.

In 1962 Ayub Khan promulgated another constitution. Presidential rather than parliamentary in focus, it was based on an indirectly elected president and a reinforced centralized political system that emphasized the country's viceregal tradition. Although Ayub anticipated launching the new political system without political parties, once the National Assembly was convened and martial law was lifted, it was apparent that political parties would be reactivated. Ayub therefore formed his own party, the Convention Muslim League, but the country's political life and its troubles were little different from the days before martial law.

Ayub Khan won another formal term as president of Pakistan in January 1965, albeit in an election in which only the Basic Democrats cast ballots. Opposed by Fatima Jinnah, the sister of Mohammed Ali Jinnah, who ran on a Combined Opposition Parties ticket, the contest was closer than expected. During the election campaign, Zulfikar Ali Bhutto who as foreign minister was supposedly a loyal member of the Ayub Khan cabinet promised in a public address that the conflict over Kashmir would be resolved during Ayub Khan's presidency. Bhutto indicated that Kashmir would be released from Indian occupation by negotiation or, if that failed, by armed force, but there was little indication that Ayub Khan had sanctioned Bhutto's pronouncement. Nevertheless, the foreign minister's speech appeared to be both solace to the pro-Kashmiri interests in West Pakistan and a green light to the Pakistan army to begin making plans for a campaign in the disputed region.

A new war over Kashmir was not long in coming. Skirmishes between Indian and Pakistani forces on the line of control between the two administrated portions of the region increased in the summer of 1965, and by September major hostilities had erupted between the two neighbours. Indian strategy confounded Pakistani plans, as New Delhi ordered its forces to strike all along the border between India and West Pakistan and to launch air raids against East Pakistan and even threaten to invade the East. Pakistan's military stores soon were exhausted, a situation made worse by an American-imposed arms embargo on both states that affected Pakistan much more than India. Ayub Khan had to consider halting the hostilities.

Ultimately, Ayub Khan was forced to accept a United Nations-sponsored cease-fire and to give up Pakistan's quest for resolving the Kashmir problem by force of arms. Embarrassed and humiliated, Ayub Khan saw all his efforts at building a new Pakistan dashed in one failed venture, and he was compelled to attend a peace conference with the Indian prime minister, Lal Bahadur Shastri, in Tashkent, in Soviet Uzbekistan. There the two leaders were unable to reach a satisfactory agreement of their own making, and their hosts compelled them to sign a draft prepared for them. At that juncture, Bhutto, who had accompanied Ayub Khan to the conference, indicated a desire to separate himself from his mentor. Ayub Khan's popularity had reached its lowest level, and, in the Pakistani game of zero-sum politics, Bhutto anticipated gaining what the president had lost. Pressed by Ayub Khan, Bhutto held up his resignation, but soon thereafter he broke with the president, joined his voice to the opposition, and in due course organized his own political party, the Pakistan People's Party (PPP).

Ayub Khan was never the same after signing the Tashkent Agreement. Confronted by rising opposition that was now led by Bhutto in West Pakistan and Mujibur Rahman in East Pakistan, Ayub Khan struck back by arresting both men. Acknowledging that he could not manage the country without a modicum of cooperation from the politicians, Ayub Khan summoned a conference of opposition leaders and withdrew the state of emergency under which Pakistan had been governed since 1965. These concessions, however, failed to conciliate the opposition, and in February 1969 Ayub announced that he would not contest the presidential election scheduled for 1970. In the meantime, protests mounted in the streets, and strikes paralyzed the economy. Sparked by grievances that could not be contained, especially in East Pakistan, the disorder spread to the western province, and all attempts to restore tranquility proved futile. One theme sustained the demonstrators: Ayub Khan had remained in power too long, and it was time for him to go.

In March 1969, Ayub Khan announced his retirement and named Gen. Agha Mohammad Yahya Khan to succeed him as president. Once again the country was placed under martial law. Yahya Khan, like Ayub Khan before him, assumed the role of chief martial-law administrator. In accepting the responsibility for leading the country, Yahya Khan said he would govern Pakistan only until the national election in 1970. Yahya Khan abolished Ayub Khan's basic democracies system and abrogated the 1962 constitution. He also issued a Legal Framework Order (LFO) that broke up the single unit of West Pakistan and reconstituted the original four provinces of Pakistan i.e., Punjab, Sind, North-West Frontier Province, and Balochistan. The 1970 election therefore was not only meant to restore parliamentary government to the country, it was also intended to reestablish the provincial political systems. The major dilemma in the LFO, however, was that in breaking up the one-unit system, the distribution of seats in the National Assembly would be apportioned among the provinces on the basis of population. This meant that East Pakistan, with its larger population, would be allotted more seats than all the provinces of West Pakistan combined.

From disunion through the Zia al-Huq era
Civil war
Pakistan's first national election therefore proved to be no panacea. After campaigning on autonomy for East Pakistan, Mujibur Rahman's Awami League won almost every seat in the National Assembly that had been allotted to the east wing under the LFO. Sheikh Mujib, as he

was popularly known, now was the paramount leader in East Pakistan, and, because his party had won a majority of the 300 contested seats in the National Assembly, Mujib was entitled to form the national government. However, Bhutto whose PPP had won a commanding majority in West Pakistan and the military establishment refused a government where the country's future might be unilaterally decided by the East. Arguing that Mujib did not have a single seat in the western provinces and that he, Bhutto, was the only serious representative from the west wing, Bhutto insisted on using another formula to organize the civilian government.

Yahya Khan was called to mediate between Mujib and Bhutto, and in the meantime their respective parties addressed the dilemma and sought still another avenue that might produce a compromise solution. Mujib, having been elected on the promise of pursuing autonomy in East Pakistan, was unwilling to compromise on his six-point program for the East to enjoy increased self-governance. Bhutto and his associates, meanwhile, saw the program as an end to federation altogether. Bhutto convinced Khan to postpone the convening of the National Assembly as the two sides worked to find a solution, and Khan did so on March 1, 1971.

Mujib declared that the people of Bengal had once again been betrayed by the power in West Pakistan. Provoked by the more radical elements in the Awami League and swept along by street demonstrations, strikes, and violent protests, he called for a boycott and general strike throughout East Pakistan. Mayhem ensued, as Bengalis attacked members of the non-Bengali community, particularly the Biharis (refugees from India and their descendants), resulting in considerable loss of life. In mid-March Khan and Bhutto again flew to Dhaka and pursued negotiations once more. At the same time, the army was being prepared for a campaign to neutralize a budding rebellion and save the unity of Pakistan.

The army struck against the Awami League and its supporters on the night of March 25, 1971. Mujib was arrested and flown secretly to a prison in West Pakistan. Other major members of the party were likewise apprehended or went into hiding. Dhaka University was fired upon, and a large number of Bengali students and intellectuals were taken into custody; scores were transported to a remote location outside the city and summarily executed. Bengali armed resistance, which came to be called the Mukhti Bhini ("Freedom Force"), took form from disaffected Bengalis in the Pakistan army and others who were prepared to fight what they now judged to be an alien army. The independent state of Bangladesh was proclaimed, and a government in exile took root in India just across the East Pakistani border.

The escalation of violence provoked a mass movement of people, the majority of whom sought refuge in India. Although this heavy influx of refugees included a good portion of the Hindus who had remained in

East Bengal after partition, many were Muslims. In fact, although the Pakistan army argued that Hindus from both portions of Bengal were responsible for the intensity of the struggle, there was no mistaking the great number of Muslim Bengalis who were being assaulted. The Pakistan army was unable to quell the fighting, and Indian forces began to supply the Mukhti Bhini. In December 1971 the Indian army invaded East Pakistan and in a few days forced the surrender of the 93,000-man West Pakistani garrison there.

Unable to supply its forces in the East, Pakistan opted not to expand the war in the West. The United States stood with Pakistan in the debate in the United Nations Security Council. Nevertheless, the U.S. government made no serious attempt to intervene and noted that its alliances with Pakistan did not commit Americans to take sides in a civil war, even one internationalized by the Indian invasion of East Pakistan. It was clear that India had effectively and irreversibly dismembered Pakistan and that the Muslim country would now take a different form from the one created by Mohammed Ali Jinnah and the Muslim League.

Zulfikar Ali Bhutto

Forced to yield his authority by the junta that had earlier sustained him, Yahya Khan resigned the presidency on December 20, 1971; unlike his predecessor, Ayub Khan, he was in no position to pass the office to still another general. The Pakistan army had suffered a severe blow, and for the time the military was content to retire from politics and rebuild its forces and reputation. Bhutto, the leading politician in what remained of Pakistan, assumed the presidency and was called to assemble a new government. Under pressure to restore equilibrium, Bhutto pledged a new Pakistan, a new constitution, and a new public order, and he articulated a vision for Pakistan that rallied diverse elements and seemed to promise a new life for the country. But the joining together of hands did not last long. Bhutto's manner, posture, and performance were more of the aristocrat than of the "Leader of the People" (Quaid-e Awam), a title he assumed for himself. In 1973 a new constitution, crafted by Bhutto and his colleagues, was adopted that restored parliamentary government. Bhutto stepped down from the presidency, which he deemed ceremonial in the new constitutional system, and assumed the more dynamic premiership.

As prime minister, Bhutto demanded nothing less than absolute power, and, increasingly suspicious of those around him, he formed the Federal Security Force (FSF), the principal task of which was his personal protection. In time, the FSF emerged as a paramilitary organization, and Bhutto's demand for ever-increasing personal security raised questions about his governing style. It also opened rifts in the PPP, and it was not long before the suspicious Bhutto ordered the silencing and imprisonment of his closest associates. The younger generation, which had idolized Bhutto during his rise to power, also became the target of police and FSF crackdowns, which often paralyzed operations at the universities. Though Bhutto had presided over the promulgation of the 1973 constitution, too much had transpired and much more unpleasantness lay ahead to conclude that the new political order could save Pakistan from repeating past mistakes.

Bhutto scheduled the country's second national election in 1977. With the PPP being the only successful national party in the country, nine opposition parties formed the Pakistan National Alliance (PNA) and agreed to run as a single bloc. Fearing the possible strength of the PNA, Bhutto and his colleagues plotted an electoral strategy that included unleashing the FSF to terrorize the opposition. However, PNA members refused to be intimidated and centred their attacks on Bhutto and the PPP by running on a particularly religious platform. Arguing that Bhutto had betrayed Islamic practices, the PNA called for a cleansing of the body politic and a return to the basic tenets of Islamic performance.

The PNA, despite their efforts, was soundly defeated in the election, but the polling had not been without incident. Almost immediately complaints arose of electoral fraud, and voter discontent soon degenerated into violent street demonstrations. Bhutto and his party had won by a landslide, but it turned out to be an empty victory. With riots erupting in all the major metropolitan areas, the army, increasingly disenchanted with Bhutto, again intervened in Pakistan's politics. Ignoring the election results, the army arrested Bhutto and dissolved his government. The prime minister was placed under house arrest, and, on July 5, 1977, Gen. Mohammad Zia ul-Haq, Bhutto's personal choice to head the Pakistan army, took the reins of government. Zia declared his intention to hold a new round of elections that would be fairer and more transparent. However, it soon became apparent that the army had no intention of allowing Bhutto to return to power. Bhutto's subsequent arrest on charges that he ordered the assassination of a political rival, and Zia's insistence that he be tried for this alleged crime, brought an end to the Bhutto era and ushered in the Zia ul-Haq regime.

Zia ul-Haq

Zia ul-Haq's initial declaration that he would return government to civilian hands was at variance with his behaviour. His subsequent change in direction hinted that there were powers behind the scene that were determined to eliminate Bhutto as an active player. Zia in fact called for a complete change in direction once the decision was made not to conduct new elections, to arrest and try Bhutto, and, ultimately, to ignore the pleadings from the governments of other countries to spare Bhutto's life. Found guilty and sentenced to death, Bhutto was hanged on April 4, 1979.

After Bhutto's death, Zia ul-Haq, president since 1978, settled to the task of redesigning a political system for Pakistan. A devout Muslim, Zia believed that religious tradition should guide Pakistan's institutions in all aspects of daily life. Moreover, the Soviet Union's invasion of Muslim Afghanistan in December 1979 reinforced Zia's belief that only by drawing from Islamic practices could the Muslims inhabiting both Pakistan and Afghanistan find common ground in their struggle to withstand the assault from an alien and aggressive neighbour. Islamization therefore became the guiding principle in Zia's plan to reform Pakistan, to reassure its unity, and to galvanize the country to meet all threats, both foreign and domestic. Clearly, the program of Islamization was also geared to reinforce the rule of Zia ul-Haq as well as establish his legitimacy.

Pakistan's status as a "frontline state" after the Soviets had invaded Afghanistan demanded a military presence, and Zia ul-Haq played a major role in assisting the Afghan resistance (the mujahideen). The country also opened its doors to an influx of several million Afghan refugees, the majority of whom were housed in camps not far from the border. The main Afghan resistance leaders also established their headquarters in and around the northern city of Peshawar. However, Pakistan had limited resources with which to assist the refugees or the Afghan mujahideen, and assistance was sought from other Muslim states, especially Saudi Arabia. After Ronald Reagan became president of the United States in 1981, Washington also answered the call for help. Pakistan soon became the third largest recipient of U.S. military aid, which by the end of Reagan's second term had reached several billion dollars. Not insignificantly, Reagan also waived all trade restrictions on aid to Pakistan, even though Islamabad was known to be pursuing an aggressive program to develop nuclear weapons. Thus, despite strains in their relationship, Washington and Islamabad found common ground in the Soviet-Afghan conflict. Moreover, U.S. intelligence services did not discourage their Pakistani counterparts most notably those in the Inter-Service Intelligence directorate from working in close harmony with the most radical religious movements in Afghanistan.

The 1979 revolution in Iran, which ended the Pahlavi monarchy there, dovetailed with developments in Pakistan. Sensing an Islamic renaissance that would sweep the majority of Islamic nations, Zia ul-Haq had no hesitation in promoting a political system guided by religious principles and traditions. Zia called for criminal punishments in keeping with Islamic law. He also insisted upon banking practices and economic activity that followed Islamic experience. Zia put his Islamization program to a referendum of the people in 1984 and coupled it to a vote of confidence in his presidency, a favourable outcome of which would provide him with an additional five years in office. Zia indeed won overwhelming approval, though only half of the eligible voters participated, and the opposition insisted that the vote was rigged. Zia nevertheless had received his vote of confidence, and his Islamization program continued as the central policy of his administration.

In February 1985 Zia ul-Haq allowed national and provincial assembly elections, though without the participation of political parties. Zia's opponents accused him of dictatorial tactics and asserted that the general-cum-president was only interested in neutralizing his opposition. Zia's Islamic system, they argued, was little more than a ploy aimed at acquiring still wider powers. Although the opposition called on voters to boycott the elections, it was largely ignored, and the people turned out in considerable numbers to elect new legislatures and thereby end still another extended period of martial law. Zia ul-Haq used the occasion of the convening of the national assembly to handpick Muhammad Khan Junejo, a Sindhi politician and landowner, to become the country's new prime minister.

Martial law was officially lifted in December 1985, and political parties sought to take advantage of the new conditions by reestablishing themselves. In January 1986, Junejo announced that he intended to revive and lead the Pakistan Muslim League often designated as Muslim League (J) to distinguish it from other factions attempting to access the party's legacy. Soon afterward Benazir Bhutto, the daughter of Zulfikar Ali Bhutto and head of the PPP, returned from a two-year exile abroad and was greeted by a tumultuous gathering of supporters who were eager to reclaim their party's reputation. Other political parties also reemerged during this period, but it was clear that in the contest for national political power the key rivals would be the Muslim League (J) and Bhutto's PPP.

Lifting martial law coincided with intensified conflict between the country's different ethnic communities, particularly in the commercial port city of Karachi. Tension between native Sindhis and Muslim immigrants from India (muhajirs) was an ever-present dilemma, and the formation of the Muhajir Qaumi Movement (MQM) in the mid-1980s was both a cause and a consequence of the violence that was directed against the immigrant community. The founding of the MQM and its increasingly militant posture aroused the native Sindhis as never before. The Sindhi complaint that the muhajirs enjoyed a monopoly of political and economic power in Karachi did not go unnoticed. Indeed, the violent clashes between Sindhis and muhajirs were an inevitable outcome of the failure to promote civil society, let alone to encourage deeper integration among Pakistan's ethnic groups. Moreover, violence could not be avoided when Pashtun migrants, notably Afghan Pashtuns, began moving from the frontier region to Karachi, posing still another challenge to the Sindhi as well as muhajir communities.

Still another problem involved the narcotics and weapons trade that had its roots in the North-West Frontier Province. By 1986 intercommunal violence in Karachi had reached a level not seen since partition, nor was the fighting contained to Karachi. Riots also broke out in Quetta and Hyderabad, and the government called on the army to restore law and order.

Confronting major opposition to his rule, challenged by intensified ethnic warfare, and struggling to sustain an economy confounded by mixed signals, in May 1988 Zia ul-Haq dissolved the national and provincial assemblies and dismissed the Junejo government. The president alleged that Junejo's administration reeked of corruption, that the prime minister was too weak to control profligate politicians, and that he had encouraged the political opposition to weaken Zia by undermining his administration. Zia promised the country still another national election, which would, he said, restore clean government, and in June he made himself head of a new caretaker government. Although the country was in considerable disarray, Zia pretended that everything was under control. On August 17, 1988, he was killed when his aircraft blew up in flight from Bahawalpur; the cause of the crash, which also took the life of the U.S. ambassador to Pakistan and several top-ranking Pakistani generals, has never been fully determined.

Political and social fragmentation
The first administration of Benazir Bhutto

Following Zia's death and under the prevailing law of succession, the chairman of the Senate, Ghulam Ishaq Khan, a longtime civil servant, became acting president. His first official act was to declare that the elections scheduled for November 1988 would be held as planned. The election results revealed that Benazir Bhutto's PPP had won somewhat less than half the seats in the legislature. One-fourth went to the Islamic Democratic Alliance (which claimed to represent the policies of the late general), and the remaining seats were won by independents and candidates from a number of lesser parties. Bhutto's party did well in Sind and the North-West Frontier Province, where it was able to form the provincial governments. However, the Punjab was won by the Islamic Democratic Alliance (Islami Jamhoori Itihad [IJI]), led by Nawaz Sharif, a Punjabi businessman, who became the province's chief minister.

Bhutto and her PPP had failed to win a mandate from the voters; however, the party had more seats in the national assembly than its nearest rival, and Ishaq Khan chose Bhutto to organize Pakistan's first civilian administration since the dissolution of her father's government in 1977. Thus, Ishaq Khan was formally elected president in December, and Benazir Bhutto became Pakistan's first female prime minister. Moreover, she was the first woman to head a Muslim state.

The new prime minister was in one respect fortunate. Soon after she came to power, the Soviet Union withdrew the last of its forces from

Afghanistan. On the other hand, an Afghan communist regime was still in power, and more than three million Afghan refugees remained in Pakistan. In an effort to sustain good relations with the army, which remained deeply committed to a presence in Afghanistan, Bhutto allowed the Pakistani military (now under the command of Gen. Mirza Aslam Baig) to sustain its proxy fight against the communist regime in Kabul. She also was compelled to use the military in a law-and-order campaign in Karachi, where ethnic unrest had continued unabated. Denied success in either operation, Bhutto began to challenge army strategy on the one side and simultaneously lost favour with the attentive Pakistani public on the other. Moreover, with developments in Sind unresolved, Bhutto aggravated the base of her supporters there.

Instead of acknowledging the need to form a coalition government with the IJI, Bhutto tried to force Nawaz Sharif to yield his position as chief minister of the Punjab. Sharif fought back, and Bhutto was confronted with more foes than she could manage. Unable to pass essential legislation, the Bhutto government faced charges of ineptitude and corruption, and demands for her removal were heard throughout the country. In August 1990 President Ishaq Khan could no longer ignore the situation and ruled that the PPP administration had lost the trust of the people. The Bhutto administration was dismissed, and another round of elections was scheduled for October. The PPP lost the contest, with Bhutto arguing that the elections had been rigged against her.

Bhutto was succeeded as prime minister by her Punjabi nemesis, Nawaz Sharif, but it was Ishaq Khan who had wielded extraordinary powers under the amended 1973 constitution (originally pressed by Zia ul-Haq to legitimize his authority). Thus, the viceregal tradition remained the dynamic force in Pakistani politics. Moreover, Bhutto's earlier dismissal of Lieut. Gen. Hamid Gul the powerful head of Inter-Service Intelligence and a close associate of President Ishaq Khan suggested that there was much behind-the-scenes maneuvering that forced the president to act. Therefore, although the election had denied Bhutto's return to the prime minister's office, it was the prevailing view that the upper echelon of the Pakistani army had had enough of Bhutto.

The first administration of Nawaz Sharif

Nawaz Sharif rode to power on a wave of anti-PPP sentiment that included that of many disenchanted PPP members. The IJI, whose central core was the revived Punjab Muslim League, now reached out to the parties dominating the politics of the North-West Frontier Province and Balochistan. Moreover, Sharif adopted Zia ul-Haq's Islamization program as his own, bolstered alliances with the religious parties, and succeeded in getting the National Assembly to approve the Shariat Bill, with its special references to the Qur'ān and Sharī'ah as the law of the land. Like Zia before him, Sharif was able to enlist the support of the Muslim orthodoxy and made its allegiance a central tenet of his rule. But while Sharif was prepared to honour the more devout members of the religious community, he could not ignore his dependency on Pakistanis in the commercial and banking world. In the end, the prime minister could not meet the expectations of his different constituencies, and his coalition crumbled. Sustained civil disobedience, acts of lawlessness, and failed economic policies produced dissatisfaction.

Despite the collapse of the communist regime in Kabul in 1992, conditions in Afghanistan remained unstable, and the Pakistani military sought to restore order by supporting an ultraconservative religious regime soon known as the Taliban that came to dominate most of strife-torn Afghanistan. Relations between the prime minister, president, and army remained problematic. Nawaz Sharif had replaced army chief of staff Baig with Gen. Asif Nawaz in 1991; but when Asif Nawaz died suddenly and somewhat mysteriously two years later, Ishaq Khan took it upon himself to appoint Lieut. Gen. Abdul Waheed Kakar his successor, without consulting the prime minister. A struggle ensued between Nawaz Sharif and Ishaq Khan, with Sharif arguing the need to eliminate the viceregal powers of the president.

In April 1993, before Sharif could act, Ishaq Khan struck back. Using his constitutional powers, the president dismissed the Sharif government and again dissolved the national assembly. Sharif appealed to the Supreme Court, claiming the president had acted arbitrarily and contrary to constitutional principle. The court unexpectedly agreed with Sharif's petition and ruled that the prime minister should be reinstated. Challenged by the unprecedented court action and acknowledging that both Sharif and Ishaq Khan had lost their credibility, the army again intervened and convinced both men that it would be in the country's interest for them to resign their respective offices in July. With both the presidency and the prime minister's office vacant, it was the army that ensured a smooth transition to still another caretaker government. Senate chairman Wasim Sajjad assumed the office of president, and Moeen Qureshi, a former World Bank official living in New York City, agreed to act as interim prime minister.

The interim government

The Moeen Qureshi administration proved to be a unique experience in the history of Pakistan. With full support from the country's armed forces, the interim prime minister moved quickly to implement reforms that included devaluing the Pakistan rupee (the national currency), exposing corrupt practices in and outside government, and demanding that monies owed the government be paid forthwith. Qureshi cracked down on the granting of public land to politicians, on the failure to pay utility bills, and on loan defaulters, who were estimated in the thousands. Insisting on austerity measures and demanding that the country learn to live within its means, his administration was a breath of fresh air in an environment known for profligacy and inefficiency. The prime minister struck a blow against the landed gentry by imposing a temporary levy on agriculture, and he made no secret of his intention to strike at the big absentee landlords and their carefully hidden sources of wealth.

Qureshi's tactics brought new funds into the Pakistan treasury, but even then they were hardly enough to return the country to solvency. Nevertheless, he persisted, even moving against the drug lords and demanding police reform so that law enforcement could more effectively deal with a deepening national problem of narcotics addiction. However, Qureshi's reforms also produced problems and a stable of critics. The devaluation of the rupee and the restrictions imposed on the country's commercial life elevated the price of gasoline, natural gas, and electricity, as well as staple food commodities. Generally speaking, though, the criticism leveled against the interim prime minister's policies emanated from the sidelined politicians who suddenly posed themselves as benefactors of the country's poorer classes.

The second administration of Benazir Bhutto
National elections were held again in October 1993. In a close contest, the PPP won a plurality though not a majority of seats in the National

Assembly; Nawaz Sharif's new Pakistan Muslim League (N) (PML-N) was a somewhat distant second, though his party received a slightly higher percentage of the popular vote. Fewer than half of registered voters cast a ballot, and election results were close throughout the country. Overall, however, Balochistan was the only province where the PPP failed to outdistance the PML-N. In alliance with Junejo's Pakistan Muslim League (J) (PML-J), the PPP formed the new civilian government, and, after three years in the opposition, Benazir Bhutto returned to the premiership.

The PML-J helped the PPP take control of the Punjab, an objective that Bhutto could not attain in her earlier administration. Nonetheless, Nawaz Sharif's party was able to form coalition provincial governments in Balochistan and the North-West Frontier Province. The power, however, was in Bhutto's hands, and it was for her to determine the country's course. Having spoken of democracy for so long, it was the prime minister's task to realize what had escaped her grasp during her previous administration. Moreover, Bhutto had the good fortune of having one of her own party, Farooq Leghari, assume the office of the president. Yet, the country remained economically unstable, and Pakistanis were far from developing a genuine civil society. Bhutto, favoured by the Americans, had to juggle relations with them and the Pakistani people: Pakistan came under U.S. pressure to freeze Pakistan's popular nuclear program and to reach a settlement over Kashmir. Furthermore, in 1993, the United States (at New Delhi's urging) had placed Pakistan on a "watch list" as a state sponsor of terrorism. India cited Islamabad's support of jihadi movements operating in Kashmir, but the Pakistani public, as well as Pakistan's military establishment, had long encouraged and supported the development of a variety of resistance groups in what they had always termed "occupied Kashmir." The U.S. pressure therefore was judged offensive and denounced by the Pakistanis.

Political crises both major and minor abounded, and Bhutto faced the added indignity of having a major family squabble spill over into the media when the prime minister's brother Murtaza Bhutto accused her husband, Asif Ali Zardari, of corruption. The incident soon spun out of control, with Bhutto's mother taking Murtaza's side. The prime minister was able to do little to push her legislative agenda, and Nawaz Sharif released documents that cited Bhutto's personal excesses; when the prime minister herself became embroiled in a banking scandal, it was almost impossible for her to mount a credible defense. President Leghari himself could not escape criticism, and it was alleged that he profited from a land deal that was linked to his PPP associations.

Bhutto, like Sharif earlier, had become bogged down responding to accusations of corruption and extortion, while the government foundered. Nationwide, chaos reigned. In Sind, another round of sectarian fighting erupted, and strife between Sunni and Shīʿite Muslims contributed to the mayhem. In the North-West Frontier Province tribal leaders had become the target of assassins, while others were implicated in trafficking weapons and drugs. The army earlier had pledged a hands-off policy in political matters, but domestic conditions had so deteriorated that that promise had to be reconsidered. Moreover, in October 1995 some 40 army officers were arrested for allegedly plotting to overthrow the government and kill the president and prime minister.

Given the intensifying woes, Bhutto no longer saw eye to eye with President Leghari, and when he ignored her advice in dealing with the army high command and with changes in the Supreme Court, their relationship reached the breaking point. Leghari, uncomfortable with the constant intrigue, was ready to take direct action against Bhutto and her husband. That moment came in September 1996, when Benazir's brother Murtaza Bhutto was killed in a police shootout, and Asif Ali Zardari was accused of complicity in Murtaza's death. In November, Leghari dismissed Bhutto's government.

The Meraj Khalid interim government was meant to keep the country on the rails, not to correct Pakistan's multidimensional problems. Bureaucrats were purged for compromising their professionalism by colluding with the PPP, the national economy underwent scrutiny by expert economists, and a serious effort was made to restore law and order. In the meantime, the politicians clamoured for a return to more-formal civilian politics. Bhutto was the most vociferous, having accused Leghari of stabbing her in the back. Ignoring these assaults, the interim government began the process of establishing a Council for Defense and National Security (CDNS), comprising the president, the prime minister, the defense minister, the interior minister, and the chairman and members of the Joint Chiefs of Staff. Although high-ranking military officers appeared favourably disposed to the formation of the CDNS, many politicians were wary and were reluctant to lend their support.

The second administration of Nawaz Sharif

Bhutto's appeal to the Supreme Court that her government had been unconstitutionally dissolved was denied, and the 1997 elections, which went forward on schedule, were judged fair in spite of claims of fraud by the PPP. Of the more than 200 seats contested in the National Assembly, the PPP won fewer than 20. Only in Sind did the PPP have anything resembling a respectable showing. The PML-N of Nawaz Sharif was the big winner, taking all the provinces either outright or through coalitions with provincial parties. Although only one-third of the eligible electorate had voted, no party in the history of Pakistan had done better in an election (taking two-thirds of the vote), and Sharif could claim a veritable mandate. With the armed forces standing by, and with the president still armed with extraordinary powers, Sharif assembled another government.

Mindful of the need to limit the power of the president, Nawaz Sharif gained parliamentary approval of the 13th amendment to the constitution, which withdrew the president's authority to remove a government at his own discretion. A 14th amendment, which prevented party members from violating party discipline, was struck down by the Supreme Court, an action that set the stage for a confrontation between the prime minister and the high court. Sharif attempted to have the number of Supreme Court members reduced from 17 to 12. However, this attempt to tamper with the judiciary stirred up the Pakistani bar, which entered the fray and demanded that Sharif be disqualified as a member of the parliament. Although the prime minister relented, by December 1997 Sharif, with assistance from the parliament, had extended his powers to such a degree that even President Leghari was forced to resign. Sharif also accrued enough power to relieve the chief justice of the Supreme Court of his duties.

Continuing challenges: conflict, a stalled economy, and nuclear tests

Nevertheless, Nawaz Sharif's successful power plays were minimized by his failure to halt the sustained ethnic conflict in Karachi and Sind, the sectarian bloodshed that had broken out in the North-West Frontier Province, and the tribal struggle for greater autonomy in

Balochistan. All of these conflicts had escalated throughout his time in office. Moreover, the government could arrest radicals and others accused of perpetuating the general disorder, but it could not bring an end to civil strife and it certainly could not act without the services provided by the army.

Sharif also had to confront an economy in shambles, and serious consideration was given to selling public assets (e.g., power stations, telecommunications, airlines, banks, and railroads) to meet obligations on the ever-growing foreign debt. Indeed, Sharif's interest in a form of "supply side" economic reorganization and privatization was not the sought-after remedy.

Despite these failures, however, by 1998 Nawaz Sharif had amassed more power than any previous elected civilian government in Pakistan. The country was a long way from achieving real growth, however, and the continuing reluctance to allow for a loyal opposition made a mockery of the regime's democratic goals. The PML-N leader used his influence to implement "Program 2010," which centred attention on education reform, the launching of public service committees, and the opening of new employment opportunities. However, the prime minister's economic program came to nothing when the countries that had been expected to provide the funding for the different ventures withdrew their offers after Pakistan detonated a series of nuclear devices in May 1998.

News of the nuclear tests sent distress signals throughout the world, and concerns only intensified with Pakistan's growing instability and the likelihood that nuclear weapons, technology, or materials could be transferred, sold, or leaked to other countries or groups (indeed, in 2004 Abdal Qadir Khan, the head of Pakistan's nuclear program, admitted to sharing weapons technology with several countries, including Iran, North Korea, and Libya). In the final analysis, Pakistan's acquisition of nuclear weapons did little to address the social and political unrest in the country, and it was hardly a boon to the national economy or to Sharif's political future.

Growing unrest, tension with the military, and Sharif's ouster

Confronted with growing unrest, much of it directed against his rule, Sharif proclaimed a state of emergency, which enabled him to rule the country by ordinance and special decrees. He also made closer alliances with the orthodox Islamic groups (e.g., the Islamic Assembly) and seemed to placate the religious divines by adopting additional Islamic laws (e.g., its punishment for adultery). A proposed 15th amendment to the constitution, establishing Islamic law as the basis of all governance, was never fully ratified, but Pakistan's Federal Shariat Court, instituted during the Zia years, was given greater latitude in meting out Islamic justice.

The prime minister's autocratic behaviour only intensified local and provincial resistance. The PPP and a number of smaller parties formed the Pakistan Awami Itehad, but it was not clear how they expected to challenge the administration. Moreover, the government had muzzled the press and ignored virtually all constitutional constraints, and administration expenditures had gone unchecked, as profligate spending on the regime's pet projects caused more severe economic dislocation. With ethnic strife continuing unabated, Pakistan's army chief of staff, Gen. Jehangir Karamat, spoke for a frustrated public when he appeared to indicate the country was teetering at the abyss. However, Karamat's role in the political process angered Nawaz Sharif, and in October 1998 the prime minister pressured the army high command into forcing the general's early retirement. Karamat was quickly and quietly replaced by Gen. Pervez Musharraf, a muhajir (post-partition immigrant) whom Sharif believed would be more compliant as well as apolitical.

Military leaders were now even more convinced that Sharif was attempting to politicize the army, but the army also had other concerns. In mid-1999 the conflict over the Kashmir region flared again, when fighting broke out with Indian forces in the high mountains of the Kargil region. The prime minister, sensing danger, made a hurried trip to Washington and appeared to yield to U.S. Pres. Bill Clinton's suggestion that Pakistani forces pull back from the contested area. However, Pakistan's generals opposed a retreat strategy, believing that the advantages favoured their forces. Most important, General Musharraf vehemently defended and stood with his fellow officers, and the impression circulated that the generals were planning to challenge Sharif's powers. Sharif, only now realizing he had made the wrong choice to head the army, set in motion a plan to replace Musharraf with another general. Musharraf, however, had the support of his fellow officers and, unlike Karamat, had no intention of yielding his position.

On October 12, 1999, Sharif attempted to oust Musharraf while the general was out of the country, but other generals thwarted the plot and arrested Sharif. On his return to Pakistan that same day, Musharraf announced the dissolution of the Sharif government and the suspension of the constitution. Although the action was clearly a coup d'état, Musharraf did not declare martial law, and he stated that fundamental rights guaranteed by the constitution were to be preserved and that all laws other than the constitution would continue in force unless altered by military authority. Musharraf nevertheless did declare a Proclamation of Emergency, and on October 14 he announced that Pres. Mohammad Rafique Tarar would remain in office, while the national and state legislatures would be suspended. The country's courts would continue operating with the limitation that the justices not interfere with any order coming from the chief executive as Musharraf at first styled himself. Moreover, Provisional

Constitution Order No. 1 of 1999 specified that the president could only act in accordance with and with the advice of the chief executive.

The Pervez Musharraf government

As chief executive, Musharraf arrogated virtual total power to himself. The general cited the substantial turmoil in the country and noted that institutions had been systematically destroyed, that the economy was in a state of near collapse, and that only the most drastic measures could even begin to improve the national condition. Musharraf said Pakistan was at a critical crossroads and that the Sharif government had even planned to split and weaken the armed forces. Noting that he could not save both the country and the constitution at the same time, Musharraf chose to sacrifice the latter for the former. Nonetheless, the constitution had not been abrogated merely held in "abeyance" until better times again allowed for its reinstatement. Careful to point out that martial law had not been imposed, he nevertheless insisted the country could not afford to perpetuate the old politics.

A Chief Executive Secretariat was hurriedly assembled in the waning days of 1999, and by mid-2000 that temporary edifice had undergone restructuring in order to give more administrative powers to the new regime. Ranking military officers assumed the most important positions in the government, and all civilian members of the secretariat had to pass scrutiny by army officers. The massive induction of serving military officers in the secretariat also was aimed at providing Musharraf with the same command and discipline structure found in the Pakistan army. The major dilemma facing Pakistan's new rulers, however, was their lack of experience in civil affairs. Moreover, on-the-job training in the day-to-day life of the country quickly caused strains within the services.

Nawaz Sharif was arrested, charged and tried for high crimes, and, after being found guilty, sentenced to a long prison term. However, under international pressure he subsequently was released and sent into exile (Saudi Arabia), with the understanding that he would remain out of the country for 10 years.

Relations with the United States, consolidation of Musharraf's rule, and meetings with India

The actions of Pakistan's generals were coldly received by many in the outside world. Washington was quick to criticize the coup leaders, and Clinton signaled his disfavour by altering his March 2000 South Asian itinerary so as to spend only a few hours in Pakistan while stopping in India and Bangladesh for longer visits. However, the strain in U.S.-Pakistan relations was caused by a wide array of issues: Pakistan's sustained political instability, its repeated failure at constructing civil society, the impediments to a resolution of the Kashmir question, and most significantly what seemed to be the country's nuclear arms race with India.

As was the case in previous military governments, Musharraf's announced intent was to return Pakistan to civilian rule as soon as feasible. The chief executive's plan to achieve this goal was similar in certain aspects to that put forward by Ayub Khan a generation earlier. Civilian rule had fragmented, and a return to full civilian control would first require the establishment of local democracy hearkening back to Ayub Khan's "basic democracies" a system devoid of competitive political parties. However, like the generals before him, Musharraf chose in June 2001 to consolidate his power by forcing the retirement of President Rafique Tarar, dispensing with the title of chief executive, and making himself president. The general also effectively became head of government, since the position of prime minister had been vacant since Sharif's ouster.

In July, as president, Musharraf traveled to Agra, India, where he met with Indian Prime Minister Atal Bihari Vajpayee to discuss regional security and, importantly, the status of Kashmir. No real progress was made, but the meeting set the stage for subsequent summit meetings between Musharraf and his Indian counterparts. The president appeared to be slipping into a role that promised a period of reflection on how to reconstruct the country's domestic and foreign policy, but that all was changed within two months by the new reality created by the September 11 attacks on the United States.

Hesitant rejection of Islamist militants

Following Pakistan's humiliating defeat in (and loss of) East Pakistan and Zia ul-Huq's subsequent emphasis on Islamization, the Pakistani army increasingly had been inclined to define its purpose in spiritual terms. Musharraf, long a key planner in Pakistan's military hierarchy, was linked to these trends. Initially, this constituted recruiting Islamist militants for clandestine operations in the Kashmir region. With the Soviet invasion of Afghanistan in 1979, Pakistan particularly the Federally Administered Tribal Areas (FATA) along the Afghan border became a safe haven for such militants from all parts of the world. The Pakistani military's Inter-Service Intelligence Directorate (ISI) became the main conduit of the country's support of the Afghan mujahideen fighters based there in their conflict with the Soviet forces in Afghanistan. Such assistance continued following the withdrawal of Moscow's forces in the late 1980s, and the ISI was instrumental in raising the Taliban as a counterforce to the rival groups seeking control of the Afghan state at that time the strategy being to give Pakistan a dominant role in Afghanistan as that country emerged from two decades of constant warfare.

Pakistan's political landscape changed dramatically with the events of September 11. It was quickly determined that the attacks on the United States had been staged by the Muslim militant organization al-Qaeda, which was operating out of Afghanistan near the Pakistani border with the support of the Taliban regime. Pakistan had diplomatic relations with Afghanistan, but Musharraf hesitated to put pressure on the Taliban to arrest al-Qaeda leader Osama bin Laden. However, as al-Qaeda and the Taliban became judged a single entity, the United States demanded Pakistani assistance as it prepared to move militarily against both organizations. Musharraf chose to side with the U.S.-led coalition against the Taliban.

Musharraf's decision to join the American effort was met with outrage by Islamist conservatives in Pakistan. Thousands of pro-Taliban Pakistani volunteers crossed the border to help in the fight against U.S. troops and their coalition allies when those forces invaded and occupied Afghanistan in the fall of 2001. In the period following the September 11 attacks and the U.S. invasion of Afghanistan, the population of Islamist militants boomed in the FATA, as Taliban and al-Qaeda fighters found refuge over the border in Pakistan. Many more Muslim recruits flocked to the FATA from abroad, eager to join the conflict.

Musharraf was pressured by Washington to take aggressive action against these Islamist operatives in the tribal areas, and the Pakistani military launched a major campaign to combat militants, particularly in mountainous Waziristan. However, the tribal Pashtun region historically had been off-limits to the central government, and Pakistan's military action not only challenged Pashtun tribal autonomy there, but it also affected members of the Pashtun community not involved with the militants. When government forces were met with stiff resistance, the soldiers often paramilitary and recruited from similar tribal orders refused to fight or fought with little enthusiasm. Musharraf dismissed a number of army officers deemed sympathetic to the Taliban, and numerous foreign jihadists (including al-Qaeda militants) were arrested by Pakistani authorities and turned over to coalition officials, but the United States continued to accuse Islamabad (and particularly Musharraf) of not doing enough to contain the terrorist threat.

Reinstated constitution

In April 2002 Musharraf, seeking to formalize his position as the head of state, held and overwhelmingly won a referendum granting him an additional five years as president. The referendum also reinstated the constitution, though modified with provisions spelled out in a document called the Legal Framework Order (LFO). In addition to extending Musharraf's term, the LFO expanded the president's powers and increased the number of members of both houses of the legislature. Parliamentary elections followed in October under the limitations imposed by the LFO, and Musharraf's adopted political party, the Pakistan Muslim League (Q) (PML-Q), took more of the seats in the National Assembly than any other contending party. The party subsequently forged a coalition government headed by PML-Q leader Mir Zafarullah Khan Jamali, a veteran politician and former Nawaz

Sharif supporter. The opposition PPP polled next highest, but it was a coalition of religious parties known as the Muttahida Majlis-e-Amal (MMA) that made the most notable showing marking the first time a Pakistani religious organization had gained a significant voice in parliament. The MMA was vehemently opposed to Musharraf's policy of confronting Islamist groups, and, after gaining a dominant political role in the North-West Frontier Province, the MMA openly questioned the army's actions in Waziristan.

Musharraf's government had been combating religious extremism at home, banning some of the more militant groups that had long been active in Pakistan and rounding up hundreds of religious activists. However, Musharraf generally had not addressed Islamist violence in Kashmir. Low-level fighting and skirmishing took place along the line of control there until late November 2003, when, unexpectedly, the Pakistani government declared a unilateral cease-fire and sought negotiations with New Delhi. The following month, two attempts were made on the president's life. Acts of political and religious violence continued to escalate, particularly those between Sunni and Shī'ite factions. Late in December the parliament ratified most provisions of the LFO as the 17th amendment to the constitution, confirming Musharraf's power to dismiss a prime minister, dissolve the National Assembly, and appoint chiefs of the armed forces and provincial governors.

In January 2004 Musharraf sought and received an unprecedented vote of confidence from a parliamentary electoral college. In August Shaukat Aziz, a former banker and minister of finance, took the premiership. Musharraf, however, clearly continued to hold the reins of power, and, despite repeated promises to return the country to full civilian authority, he announced at the end of the year that the country was too fragile for him to comply with his own deadlines. This applied also to the president's refusal to step down as head of the armed forces, despite repeated demands by political opponents that he do so. On the other side of the political spectrum, Musharraf had to contend with constant attacks from the MMA, who accused him of seeking to secularize Pakistan. The country continued to be subject to increasing incidents of sectarian violence, including suicide bombings at mosques and other public places. Adding to this human-generated calamity, Pakistan suffered a devastating earthquake in October 2005 in the Kashmir region that killed tens of thousands of people and left hundreds of thousands homeless.

Electoral losses and resignation

In early 2007 Musharraf began seeking reelection to the presidency. However, because he remained head of the military, opposition parties and then the Pakistan Supreme Court objected on constitutional grounds. In March Musharraf dismissed Chief Justice Iftikhar Mohammad Chaudhry, which sparked a general strike of

Pakistani lawyers and outbreaks of violent protest in various parts of the country; the Supreme Court overturned the dismissal in July, and Chaudhry was reinstated. In October an electoral college consisting of the parliament and four provincial legislatures voted to give Musharraf another five-year term, although opposition members refused to participate in the proceedings. After the Supreme Court delayed the pronouncement of this outcome (in order to review its constitutionality), Musharraf declared a state of emergency in early November. The constitution was once again suspended, members of the Supreme Court (including Chaudhry) were dismissed, and the activities of independent news media organizations were curtailed. Later in the month, the Supreme Court, reconstituted with Musharraf appointees, upheld his reelection; Musharraf subsequently resigned his military commission and was sworn into the presidency as a civilian.

In the fall of 2007 Nawaz Sharif and Benazir Bhutto who had also been living in exile were permitted to return to Pakistan, and each began campaigning for upcoming parliamentary elections scheduled for early January 2008. At the end of December, however, Bhutto was assassinated at a political rally in Rawalpindi, an act that stunned Pakistanis and set off riots and rampages in different parts of the country. Musharraf, having only just lifted the state of emergency, had to again place the armed forces on special alert, and he was forced to postpone the election until mid-February.

The outcome of the voting was seen as a rejection of Musharraf and his rule; his PML-Q party finished a distant third behind the PPP (now led by Asif Ali Zardari, Bhutto's widower), which captured about one-third of the parliamentary seats up for election, and Sharif's party, the PML-N, with about one-fourth of the seats. In March the PPP and PML-N formed a coalition government. Yousaf Raza Gilani, a prominent member of the PPP and a former National Assembly speaker, was elected prime minister.

Disagreements emerged within the governing coalition in the months following its formation, particularly regarding the reinstatement of the Supreme Court judges Musharraf had dismissed late the previous year, and these disputes threatened to destabilize the alliance. Nevertheless, in August 2008 the coalition moved to begin impeachment charges against Musharraf, citing grave constitutional violations; on August 18, faced with the impending proceedings, Musharraf resigned.

Pakistan under Zardari

Conflict within the coalition continued to escalate following Musharraf's departure. In light of ongoing differences, including disputes over Musharraf's successor, Sharif subsequently withdrew the PML-N from the governing coalition and indicated that his party would put forth its own candidate in the presidential elections announced for early September; however, neither the PML-N nor the PML-Q candidate won enough support to pose a challenge to Zardari, the PPP's candidate, and on September 6, 2008, he was elected president.

Friction between Zardari and Sharif intensified in early 2009 when the Supreme Court voted to disqualify Sharif's brother from his position as chief minister of the Punjab and to uphold a ban prohibiting Sharif himself from holding political office (the ban stemmed from his 2000 conviction for high crimes). Sharif alleged that the court's rulings were politically motivated and backed by Zardari. In addition, the status of the Supreme Court judges dismissed under Musharraf who had yet to be reinstated one of the issues that had undermined the Sharif-Zardari coalition remained a major source of conflict between the two rivals. In March 2009 Sharif broke free of an attempt to place him under house arrest and headed toward the capital, where he planned to hold a rally advocating for the reinstatement of the judges. Faced with this prospect, the government agreed to reinstate Chief Justice Chaudhry and a number of other Supreme Court judges who had not yet been returned to their posts. The move was seen as a political victory for Sharif and a significant concession on the part of Zardari, who is thought to have opposed Chaudhry's return because of the possibility that the amnesty Zardari had received under Musharraf might be overturned. Shortly thereafter, Sharif's brother was also returned to his position, and the ruling that banned Sharif from holding office was lifted in May.

U.S. drone strikes, floods of 2010, and religious tensions

Meanwhile, against the backdrop of the political drama of 2008, there were also developments on the foreign relations front. That year the United States expanded its campaign of targeted killings by remotely piloted drones in Pakistan's Federally Administered Tribal Areas, a region known to be a haven for Pashtun militants waging a guerilla war against international forces and the Afghan government in Afghanistan. The drone strikes, which had begun in 2004 under the direction of the Central Intelligence Agency with the silent approval of the Pakistani government, stirred up widespread public outrage in Pakistan as they increased in frequency and caused increasing numbers of civilian deaths and injuries. Although Pakistani leaders decried the strikes as violations of Pakistan's sovereignty, there continued to be reports of the government's secret cooperation. Later that year, limited trade between the Pakistani- and Indian-administered portions of Kashmir resumed. It was the first such commerce in more than 60 years and signaled improved relations between the two countries.

In the summer of 2010 Pakistan faced the most destructive floods in the country's recorded history. Swollen by unusually heavy monsoon rains, the Indus River which in a typical monsoon season can expand to more than half a mile (one kilometre) by the time it reaches the provinces of Punjab and Sindh grew to some 15 times its normal breadth. By mid-August more than 1,500 Pakistanis had died as a result of the river's extraordinary flooding, and, with some one-fourth of the country touched by the floods, many millions more were affected to various degrees. The humanitarian disaster caused by the flooding was marked by shortages of food and drinking water, the threat of waterborne disease, looting and violence, and the disruption of transportation and communications infrastructure. In a country so reliant upon its agriculture, the inundation which submerged swaths of cropland and killed large populations of livestock promised to have a lasting effect on the production of food and of raw materials such as cotton, which sustains the country's export-heavy textile industry.

Religious tensions reappeared in January 2011 with the assassination of the governor of Punjab province, Salman Taseer, by a member of his own security detail. Taseer, a member of the PPP and a political ally of Zardari, had been among the most vocal critics of Pakistan's blasphemy law, which called for the death penalty if a defendant was convicted of defaming Islam or Muhammad. Although the law, which was established in the 1980s under Zia ul-Haq's Islamization program, had not resulted in any executions for blasphemy, it had become a point of contention between religious conservatives and secular politicians. Taseer's assassination, carried out by an elite police commando with a history of Islamic radicalism, raised fears that moderate politicians were vulnerable to intimidation by religious conservatives. The public reaction to the assassination further highlighted the divisions in Pakistani society; while the PPP and most other political parties condemned the attack, many religious leaders and organizations denounced Taseer as an apostate and praised his killer for defending Islam.

Osama bin Laden discovered and killed

On May 2, 2011, a U.S. military operation in Pakistan killed Osama bin Laden, the leader of the al-Qaeda network. The assault, carried out by a small team transported by helicopter, was launched after U.S. intelligence located bin Laden living in a walled compound in Abbottabad, a medium-sized city near Islamabad. Bin Laden's presence in Abbottabad threatened to add new tension to the often-troubled security alliance between the United States and Pakistan. Pakistani officials had often denied claims that bin Laden was hiding out in Pakistan, possibly abetted by Islamic militants in the remote and rugged areas on the Afghan border. After bin Laden's death, the news that he had in fact lived in a large compound in an affluent area near the Pakistan Military Academy, one of the country's most prestigious military institutes, raised questions about how his presence could have escaped the notice of Pakistan's security forces.

Defeat at the polls

Zardari and the PPP-led governing coalition entered legislative elections in May 2013 with low approval ratings because of widespread discontent over corruption and weak economic development. The main beneficiary was Nawaz Sharif, whose reputation as a businessman and economic reformer helped the PML-N win considerably more seats than its closest challengers, the PPP and Imran Khan's Tehreek-e-Insaf (Justice Movement) party, positioning Sharif for a third term as prime minister.

The third administration of Nawaz Sharif

Domestic and foreign policy

Sharif began his third term as prime minister as a popular reformer. The economy improved substantially, with higher growth rates, a stable rupee, and lower inflation. The country's infrastructure, however, continued to face hurdles, with demand for electricity outpacing supply and resulting in frequent and widespread shortages. His foreign policy agenda was oriented toward liberalizing trade, including with Pakistan's neighbours. To do so, he made overtures for peaceful relations with India and post-NATO Afghanistan and attempted to reach a peace settlement with the Tehrik-e-Taliban Pakistan (TTP), an Islamist insurgency operating in Pakistan and unaffiliated with the Taliban in neighbouring Afghanistan.

Under Sharif, Pakistan saw significant investment from China as the flagship program of China's "Belt and Road Initiative" (BRI). China lent Pakistan tens of billions of dollars in order to develop Pakistan's infrastructure and build a China-Pakistan Economic Corridor (CPEC) that would allow China access to cheaper, more efficient trade routes. One of the program's grandest projects was the development of the Gwadar seaport and a highway connecting it to China's Xinjiang province. However, with the development projects paid for through hefty loans from China that required employment of Chinese businesses, Pakistan's debt ballooned.

Disqualification from office

Sharif's foreign outreach agenda stepped on the toes of the military establishment and the opposition. When opposition protests in 2014 provided a premise for the military to oust Sharif with popular support, the military instead used the opportunity to pressure Sharif to defer to military generals on matters of foreign policy and defense.

The 2015 leak of confidential international financial documents known as the Panama Papers linked three of Sharif's children to offshore companies that they had allegedly used to purchase real estate in London. Sharif and his children denied any wrongdoing, but a corruption probe was opened into the matter. In 2017 the Supreme Court disqualified Sharif from holding public office, forcing his resignation. He was replaced by Shahid Khaqan Abbasi as prime minister. Sharif's brother Shehbaz Sharif was selected to lead the PML-N party in the next elections.

Arrest and party defeat

Sharif and his family went into exile, and in July 2018 he and his daughter Maryam Nawaz Sharif were convicted in absentia. They returned to Lahore on July 13 to serve their sentences, saying that they were giving themselves up for the people of Pakistan at a "critical juncture" ahead of the elections. They were arrested shortly after arriving.

When the elections were held in late July, Imran Khan's Tehreek-e-Insaf party appeared to outperform the PML-N. To guarantee security in the highly contentious election, the military had stationed at least 350,000 troops at the polling stations, and the Election Commission had granted the military express judicial power at those polling stations. While Khan praised the elections as the fairest in Pakistan's history, the PML-N and the other parties expressed concern that the military had interfered in the elections, especially after their poll observers were ordered to leave polling stations before votes were counted. Nonetheless, the PML-N conceded, allowing Khan to seek a coalition and become prime minister.

Imran Khan's premiership

Khan became prime minister as Pakistan faced a new debt crisis. Its debt commitments had ballooned over the previous years, not least due to the CPEC project financed by loans from China; Pakistan's first repayments were due to begin in 2019. The crisis worsened just weeks into his premiership when the United States decided to withhold $300 million in promised military aid, saying the country had not done enough to fight terrorism. Khan had campaigned on promises of increased welfare and against seeking intervention from the International Monetary Fund (IMF), whose lending conditions often required austerity measures and whose previous dozen packages to Pakistan had failed to solve the country's macroeconomic problems. Indeed, he began his premiership seeking aid from allies rather than from the IMF. In mid-October, having failed to secure foreign aid from allies, Pakistan requested $12 billion in emergency lending from the IMF. Khan continued to seek foreign aid, however, and reached investment arrangements with China in December and with Saudi Arabia and the United Arab Emirates in January 2019.

Under Khan, Pakistan saw significant developments in its foreign relations. The country made successful efforts to pressure the Taliban in Afghanistan into peace talks, improving its relations with the United States. Afghanistan's central government initially thanked Pakistan for its efforts, but diplomatic relations soured after comments by Khan undermined the authority of the central government. Tensions with

India over Kashmir came to a head in February 2019, after a suicide bombing there resulted in the deaths of 40 Indian security personnel. When a militant group believed to operate illegally in Pakistan took credit for the attack, the Indian Air Force conducted air strikes in Pakistan for the first time in five decades. Though India claimed it had destroyed a large training camp belonging to the militant group, Pakistan denied that any such camp had existed and said India had struck an empty field instead. The next day, Pakistan shot down two fighter jets from India and captured a pilot, who was soon returned to India. Despite the skirmishes, the two countries seemed to avoid further escalating the situation. Pakistan, meanwhile, began a crackdown on militants, arresting suspected militants, shutting down a large number of religious schools, and announcing its intent to update existing laws according to international standards.

The Country Guide

Sightseeing

Travel ideas for Pakistan unique sights, worth Guinness records
Hussaini Suspension Bridge
Hussaini Suspension Bridge situated in Pakistan also deserves the attention of fans of extreme entertainment. It was designed to move across the Hunza River. The current bridge is the second one. The fact is that this area is characterized by windy weather, and, therefore, the first bridge constructed of thin ropes and planks was almost

completely destroyed. Some surviving elements can still be seen next to the existing bridge, which only adds excitement to tourists.

The second bridge isn't reliable too, as it was built out of the simplest materials - ropes and planks. Hussaini Suspension Bridge is very old. Even locals can't recall the exact date of its construction. For many years, planks have broken down and gaps between the boards have become quite large. Huge holes in the bridge and icy wind that never ceases to blow make getting over Hunza incredibly dangerous. Hussaini Suspension Bridge is located near the village of the same name. As local residents recall, at least ten people were fallen while passing the bridge. It is considered the most dangerous bridge in the world, as the permanent cold wind blowing from the mountains of the Karakoram makes getting over even more dangerous.

Lahore
Pakistani fortress-city Lahore is also known all over the world. It was established thousand years ago. In the 16th-17th century it was at the top of the development. At that time Lahore was the capital of the Mogul Empire. Tourist visit this city in order to see the magnificent architectural complex Shahi Qila fortress that was built in the beginning of the 17th century in the center of the city. Several years ago this fortress was inscribed as a UNESCO World Heritage Site.

The walls of this large complex hide the landmarks of an incredible beauty. The Pearl Mosque and the Palace of Mirrors are the most splendid. After exploring the fort, you can walk in the wonderful gardens of Lahore. The Hazuri Bagh Garden is the largest. Only professional florists attend about it every day.

Lahore is well-known thanks to the Badshahi mosque, the most outstanding Muslim landmark. It was built in the Medieval period and till our days it is the second largest mosque in the country. Samadhi of Ranjit Singh has also been highlighted among other landmarks. You can order excursions not only in a daytime but also in the evening. All the buildings are decorated with marvelous illumination. Notwithstanding that facts, that Lahore has a lot of historical monuments, it is a modern city with hundreds of hotels, restaurants and shopping malls.

Lake Sheosar
In the North of Pakistan, you can find a wonderful Sheosar Lake. It was placed on the territory of Deosai National Park. The lake is world known thanks to its crystal-clear water. For hundreds of years the lake has been being the clearest reservoir on the planet. Its maximum depth goes up to 40 meters and length is about 2,3 km, width 1,8 km. The lake is situated in a remote mountain region, at a high of 4 142 metres above the sea level.

Travelers can order neither four-wheel drive nor hiking excursions in Deosai National Park. You can get to the remote mountain region in a couple of hours by the off-roader, whilst trekking will take no less than two days. Admirers of nature have to walk in the nature reserve on foot. There were made special areas where people can put a tent up and stay for a night or just to relax.

The best time for visiting the wonderful lake and walking in the reservation is from the beginning of June until the end of September. At this time a great number of flowers surround the lake and the nearby territory. Butterflies are the main peculiarity of this place. You can see several decades of the species. In November everything in the valley is covered with snow. Only in May nature completely wakes up from a deep dream. That's why during this period the reservation is closed for visitors.

Rift in Shigi
The rift in Shigi is another large earth' break up that has formed in Pakistan. This region has quite a small population that's why mass media didn't pay attention to the geological anomaly. The video was downloaded to a popular international site. Only after that, the world knew about this accident.

In the video was shown a huge rift from the beginning till the end. In some places, the width of the fault was about 50 cm and in another wasn't more than a cm. There wasn't made any official researching works and until now there is no precise data about the width and depth of the fault. The area of the fissure has quite a dry sandy soil. Rains is a rare phenomenon there, that's why such faults can't happen there naturally. The rift is situated near Gulistan city and locals knew about the geological anomaly only after the video publication.

Faisal Mosque

Faisal Mosque is the mosque in Islamabad, Pakistan. It is the largest mosque on the territory of South-Eastern Asia. In the world, it is in the fourth place in the area. This mosque doesn't look like other Pakistani mosques. A famous Turkish architect Vedat Dalokay didn't want to make traditional cupolas and created the unusual constructions that resemble a Beduin tent.

Before the building was organized an international competition in which architects from 17 countries submitted 43 proposals. Design of Vedat Dalokay was chosen as the most extraordinary and symbolic. The unusual building looked quite harmonious and unusual. Enter to the mosque you can through the inner yard that is decorated with a small artificial pond and marvellous fountains. The most beautiful marble types, delicate mosaics and calligraphic patterns were used for the inner decoration. The best masters from Pakistan did their best to decorate this mosque.

The payers hall is enormous, at once there can be up to 10 000 believers. The mosque has an additional hall for 24 000 people, the inner yard can meet up to 40 000 people. This great mosque was built within ten years and was finished in 1986. The great sum of money for the building was given by King Faisal bin Abdul Aziz. In honour of him was named not only the mosque but also the road leading to it

Badshahi Mosque

In Lahore you can see the royal Badshahi Mosque. From 1674 it is the second-largest Pakistan mosque. The building is situated on a high platform that was built especially before the mosque. The religious building has the largest inner yard in the world, its length is 527 meters and 159 widths. The minarets high is 62 meters, together all these peculiarities make this mosque magnificent.

A huge building is decorated with three white marble cupolas. Near the main entrance, there is a two-tired 20 meters pavilion. This mosque is quite extraordinary and attracts people from the whole world. There is a small museum devoted to the Islamic relics. Among them, there are some unique values the green prophet Muhammad's turban and delicate scarfs, made by his daughter Fatima.

These relics became a reason of interesting stories. Until nowadays we don't know about their appearance in the mosque. According to the main theory, they were given by the Conqueror Timur and originally, they were in Sheesh Mahal Palace. In 2002 the mosque has lost one of its relics sandals of the prophet Muhammad. After this accident, the government wanted to close the museum and take the exponents to the Lahore's museum but later was decided not to replace the relics.

City and Regions

Islamabad
Guide to Islamabad
Sightseeing in Islamabad what to see. Complete travel guide
Islamabad is a governmental center of Pakistan, a large cultural region and an attractive destination for rest. The building of the city started in 1960 in the middle of an absolute desert. It took just several decades to turn a lifeless steppe into a modern megalopolis. A famous Greek architect worked over the creation of the city. Islamabad was thoroughly planned and so it doesn't look like the majority of Middle East towns with their narrow labyrinth like streets.

There is a large number of wonderful places in Islamabad. Shah Faisal Mosque is the most interesting sight from architectural and religious points of view. The walls of this building have enough space for up to 70 thousand of people. Garden of Roses and Jasmine remains the most beautiful place of the city. Besides flower beds the park is decorated by wonderful fountains, statues and decorative bushes.

On the territory of the city are also located several lakes. The biggest ones of them are Lotus Lake, Raval and Simli. Just like any Middle East city, Islamabad has rich choice of trading squares and markets Abpara Market, Melody Market, Covered Market, Juma Bazar, and Jinnah Market. Among cultural facilities of the city the most notable ones are

Lok Virsa Museum, Pakistan Museum of Natural History and Islamabad Museum.

In the immediate vicinity of Islamabad, there is an interesting historical landmark - the Rohtas Fort. Its construction began in 1541 and lasted for two years. The fortress was built to protect the lands from the Mongol conquerors. The defensive structure is now striking in its scale; the perimeter of the fortress walls is about 4,000 meters and the height about 18 meters. The entrance to the fortress is a gate made of sandstone. The fortress lost its strategic importance in the 18th century, and several years ago it was recognized as a UNESCO World Heritage Site.

An equally interesting historical site is the archaeological district of Taxila. It was named after the eponymous town, the ruins of which were discovered by researchers in these places. This ancient Buddhist city was founded in the times of Alexander of Macedon. On its territory, there were many unique examples of architecture and sculptures, including a statue of Buddha of impressive size. Visitors of the archaeological region will have the opportunity to see fragments of an ancient monastery, and many more defensive structures that were used to protect the city.

Guests of Islamabad will have the opportunity to get to the nearby Buddhist monastery of Takht-i-Bahi, built in the 1st century BC. This monastery remained active until the 7th century. It represents a large and incredibly interesting complex of structures. Here tourists will have the opportunity to look into the old cells, see the halls in which important meetings were held, and also visit the refectory. The monastery is located on the top of the mountain. From these places, a magnificent panoramic view of the surroundings opens.

Fans of natural attractions will not be bored either as they will be able to visit the Margalla Hills National Park. The park is big and incredibly beautiful. It is home to many rare species of animals. The luckiest travelers will have an opportunity to see graceful deer during the tour. Pheasants also walk freely in the park. One day will not be enough to explore all the amazing sights of this reserve. There are several routes options for tourists. Some types of excursions are designed specifically for tourists with children.

Islamabad for Family and Kids

Family trip to Islamabad with children. Ideas on where to go with your child

There are not many entertainment centers and children's institutions in Islamabad, as in some other cities of the country. However, vacationers with children do not have to be bored here. One of the most interesting places in the city is the Pakistan Museum of Natural History. This natural-science museum is not at all like many others that one can visit in other cities. Part of its exposition is located on the adjacent territory, and a part in an indoor pavilion. Visitors can see stuffed animals, slices of age-old trees and many more unique artifacts, somehow connected with the nature of Pakistan. Children will certainly love the huge skeletons of dinosaurs and models of exotic fish. A tour of the museum promises to be very informative.

The city has a beautiful zoo called the Islamabad Zoo, which also enjoys well-deserved popularity among tourists with children. In this zoo live lions and zebras, birds of prey, as well as other exotic animals. Visitors are allowed to feed some friendly inhabitants of the zoo. Another interesting feature of the zoological garden is its decoration. On its vast territory, there are realistic figures of dinosaurs everywhere, against which, one can make a lot of interesting photos. The zoo is very large. On its territory, there are many beautiful places for walks and equipped recreation areas.

Nature lovers should definitely stroll through the picturesque Rose and Jasmine Garden. It will be difficult to find a more interesting and beautiful place to relax outdoors with children. As one can guess by the name of the garden, its main decorations are beautiful roses and jasmine shrubs, the blossoms of which can be admired every spring. The garden is very large. It contains many beautiful shops, and observation platforms from which one can admire the panorama of the city and the surrounding mountains. In the garden, there are many spacious lawns for children, where they can run and play in the shade of trees.

Another original place which is sure to appeal to young travelers is the Bird Aviary reserve. Its main inhabitants are birds, including colorful parrots, rare waterfowl breeds, beautiful pheasants and peacocks, as well as some species of birds of prey that can be found in the mountains of Pakistan. In the reserve, a large artificial lake with fountains is equipped for birds. It is beautifully decorated and occupies a rather large territory. The reserve is also noteworthy for its original design. There are pendant bridges for its visitors, thanks to which it is even more convenient to observe the birds.

With older children, one can go for a walk around the Margalla Hills reserve, which is located in an incredibly beautiful mountainous area. Many pedestrian routes of different duration are laid along its territory. During the excursion, one can walk along the most beautiful mountain forests, look into the hidden caves, and find fast flowing mountain streams and waterfalls among the thick thickets of age-old trees. A walk through the reserve is sure to please all fans of outdoor activities.

There are several entertainment centers in Islamabad that are perfect for relaxing on a hot day. One of the best is the entertainment center Megazone Islamabad. For young children, it has prepared a lot of slot machines. With older children, one can engage in bowling. Also in the entertainment center, there is an excellent cafe, so one can spend the whole day here in comfort.

Islamabad Cultural Sights

Culture of Islamabad. Places to visit old town, temples, theaters, museums and palaces

Besides the internationally famous Faisal Mosque, Rohtas Fort, and Taxila Ruins, Islamabad and surrounding regions have many interesting places that definitely deserve a visit. For example, Daman-E-Koh viewing point north of Islamabad is one of the must-visit landmarks. The incredibly beautiful area is very interesting to explore. Moreover, it also offers a truly breathtaking panorama of the city. This is a true piece of paradise on Earth, and monkeys have become sort of "inhabitants of the Eden". There are really many monkeys here, so drivers must be particularly attentive because the animals can appear on the road out of nowhere. In the park, monkeys have become one more landmark of the area.

Fans of colossal monuments will find it exciting to visit a sculpture complex named Pakistan. This is one of the symbols of the country and true national pride. The monument symbolizes three territories of Pakistan and four provinces of the country. Unity and sacrosanctity are the core ideas of the eye-catching architectural landmark. The monument is designed in a shape of flower petals. Moreover, it is a fantastic viewing point that offers a tremendous panorama of Islamabad. The nearby area is a popular destination for picnics. Young people particularly like this place.

Shrine Of Hazrat Bari Imam Sarkar is one more grandiose sacred place in the capital of Pakistan. Built in an oriental style of the Arabian architecture, this shrine is a magnet for everyone who wants to get acquainted with the local culture and learn more about the history of the city and the country. It is an incredibly peaceful place with its special atmosphere even non-Muslim people notice that. Not far from the landmark, there is a market where visitors can buy interesting items (and, of course, bargain with local sellers, which is a must during a stay in Islamabad).

The Shrine of Meher Ali Shah in Golra Sharif is one more religious landmark that is a primary destination for everyone who wants to learn more about the local culture. The mausoleum frequently hosts various religious celebrations. The landmark looks gorgeous both inside and outside, but the fabulous design is not the only reason to visit this amazing place. The shrine, just like many other mosques, has an inimitable atmosphere of tranquility and peace. The mausoleum is also a tomb of Islamic saints with their sons.

Among museums in Pakistan, there are several universal and unique establishments that will appeal to everyone. The museum located close to the Pakistan monument attracts everyone who wants to learn more about the newest history of the country starting from the Muhammad Ali Jinnah, the founder of Pakistan. Local people also like to visit this museum to feel united as a nation. Among the exhibits, there are paintings, art installations, and sculptures that describe the life of ordinary Pakistani people and officials.

Travelers interested in visiting original places that unleash the unique cultural heritage of Pakistani people will find what they want at Lok Virsa Museum. It is a great place to see and earn more about the traditional crafts of different folks that live in Pakistan. There are goods made of leather, ceramics, textile, metal. Moreover, there is a separate hall dedicated to musical instruments. The museum is usually referred to as one of the best cultural venues in the capital and the most "Pakistani" museum in Islamabad that casts the light upon the everyday life of ordinary people. In total, there are roughly 25 large galleries with interesting exhibits.

Golra Sharif Railway Museum, which is also known as Pakistan Railways Heritage Museum, is one more important destination for everyone interested in the heritage of the country. Here, visitors can see the station that once made the North-West Railway famous. Children will be particularly pleased to visit this interesting museum. The Pakistan Museum of Natural History exhibits many interesting wax figures including the giant skeleton of a blue whale. It is a place where ancient history becomes alive. Anthropology fans will be genuinely pleased to visit this place. Finally, art connoisseurs will be very excited to looks at exhibits in the National Art Gallery that has more than 450 precious artworks.

Islamabad Attractions and Nightlife

City break in Islamabad. Active leisure ideas for Islamabad attractions, recreation and nightlife

Islamabad is a city located at the foot of a mountain. It attracts hundreds of thousands of tourists with its numerous landmarks and the activities it offers, rock-climbing included. Margalla Hills is one of the best destinations for that. The names of the peaks, which are a part of the hills, are very poetic and charming - Jasmine Corner, Jungle Rock, and Legacy Wall. There are several companies that offer rock climbing tours to guests of Pakistan, and Terichmir Travel is one of the best in this field. It offers different routes depending on the wishes of its clients.

For example, Trail 2 is the best choice for everyone who wants to visit Daman-E-Koh viewing point. As this area has become home to numerous monkeys, locals informally call it "the trail of animals". The walk will take 1 2 hours. Participants reach the viewing point and then can walk somewhat further to see a hidden gem the remains of 202 AirBlue airplane. Trail 3 is the most popular choice, but travelers need to keep in mind that this trail has many stiff slopes. Having reached Daman-E-Koh, vacationers can continue their walk and visit Pir Sohawa. There are three restaurants that are great for relaxing and having a light meal. Trail 5 also reaches Pir Sohawa, but this trail is quite complex and it is easy to get lost there. That being said, it is better to explore Trail 5 together with a guide. However, experienced rangers can try to do that alone.

Rawal Lake, which is located not far from Shakar Parian National Park, is great for fishing. Such pastime is a great way to make any stay in the capital of Pakistan more exciting. Needless to say, all fans of fishing will be happy to explore a new fishing site. Rawal Dam Fishing Point offers fishing tours for all guests of the capital. In order to try rafting, simply contact Canoeing Company. Vacationers may also be interested in a cruise on the picturesque lake. For this purpose, simply contact companies like Boating Lake View or Navy Sailing Club.

At Margalla Hills, it is possible to try such activity as paragliding. Young people are usually particularly fond of it. Safaris are also on the rise these days. Jeep Safari Pakistan offers a range of safari tours in the region. Having ordered a tour from them, tourists are guaranteed to get unforgettable memories and admire stunning suburban and wild areas of Pakistan. Active Tours Pakistan and Gondogoro Treks & Tours also offer many interesting tours. Moreover, vacationers can always enjoy horse riding tours without a doubt, this is an excellent pastime that can make everyone happy.

F 1 Traxx and 2F2F Formula Karting offer an amazing opportunity to try karting in Islamabad. The nearby Laila Carnival Park is an excellent destination for tourists with children aged 3 to 6. Fans of attractions, both children and adults, are welcome at MTX Offroad Sports Rawal

Lake or Fun City. These parks are always filled with entertainment and fun. Golf fans will never feel bored in the capital as they can play their favorite game at Jinnah Driving Range or Islamabad Golf Club whenever they want. Gun & Country Club is one more venue to have fun and try something new. It is particularly appealing to everyone who likes shooting and wants to polish own accuracy. That said, Battlefield Club is also an amazing destination for fans of shooting.

Bahria Enclave Zoo is one more place that definitely deserves a visit. That is particularly true about tourists with children. At the zoo, it is possible to see many different species that belong to the cat family lions, tigers, leopards, and cougars. The zoo is not big; nevertheless, it is a wonderful place, a visit to which will be surely unforgettable. In the city, there is one more zoo that has a very simple name, Islamabad Zoo. It has become home to animals of different species: mountain goats, elephants, peacocks, eagles, zebras, and lions. There are also interesting sculptures of dinosaurs, crocodiles, and giant reptiles. These are not all zoos in Islamabad. There is also Bird Aviary that, as it is not hard to guess by its name, is a great destination for everyone who wants to look at various birds.

In order to see new films, consider visiting Centaurus Cineplex or JFC Cineplex. When you are in a mood for peaceful relaxation in a tranquil area, beautiful parks in Islamabad are the best choice. Lake View Park is a wonderful destination for everyone who wants to sit here and enjoy the cool weather. Famous for its lush flora, Shakarpariyan Hills is an ideal place to enjoy mesmerizing views of Pakistan's capital. It is also a wonderful destination for the whole family. Moreover, the park itself is a historical landmark - Shakarpariyan Hills is one of the oldest parks in the city.

It would be a mistake to say that Islamabad has as many nightclubs and bars as, let's say, Las Vegas. However, it still has several attractive venues that travelers will find interesting to visit. Everyone, who wants to eat a delicious dinner and enjoy cozy and trouble-free atmosphere, shouldn't pass B.Q. Tonight Bar by. Le Casa Del Habanos is a perfect choice for everyone who likes restaurants with live music, and Burn Out is suitable for all tourists who simply want to relax in a casual atmosphere. Somalian Centre pleased with its fabulous choice of spirits. If you want to play billiards and spend several hours enjoying the game, Breaker's Snooker Club is the right choice.

Islamabad Cuisine and Restaurant

Cuisine of Islamabad for gourmets. Places for dinner best restaurants

Islamabad cuisine has its own peculiarities defined by the geographic location of the country. Pakistan is a kind of interlink between India and the Middle East, and both regions have influenced local cuisine, creating something really unique. Rice, meat, and spices are the main ingredients in Pakistani cuisine. For travelers, it will be very interesting to try Samosa (patty cakes with various fillings), Tikka (beef grilled on coals), Shish Kebab and Shami Kebab (Pakistani kebabs), Dum Pukht (boiled mutton with spices), Kofta (meatballs), Pulau (boiled rice with meat), Korma (meat curry), Gosht Hara Masala (marinated meat stew with spices).

The cuisine of the Middle East is a true paradise for sweet tooths. Pakistani cuisine is no exception. It features all kinds of sweets and desserts. Among the most popular delights, it is important to mention Barfi (milk and coconut candy), Mitai (candy with milk, flour, and syrup), Firni (rice and milk pudding), Halva (dessert made with nuts, cream, carrots, and eggs), and Raita (creamy paste). Tea is the most popular drink here, and it is available in different variations, such as tea with spices, milk, sugar, and lemon. Lassi (a yogurt-based drink) is also very popular. When it comes to alcoholic beverages, tourists prefer to order Arak (anise vodka) and locally brewed beer.

Everyone will easily find a suitable restaurant or a café in the capital of Pakistan that will fit all requirements. For example, if you want to enjoy nutritious and inexpensive food, such restaurants as Pizza Party (as it is not hard to guess, this restaurant specializes in pizza), Bismillah Tikka and Chargha House (a great place to try Pakistani cuisine), Tapas Restaurant (mostly serves Spanish cuisine), and Savour Foods (offers simple and delicious food) will definitely please their visitors.

For sweet tooths, the capital of Pakistan has prepared many interesting restaurants and cafes, a visit to which will be very exciting. These are Burning Brownie famous for its casual atmosphere and original desserts; Gelato, which is like a magnet for all fans of ice cream; and Hotspot that is often considered the best place to try cakes and patty cakes. Fans of fine cuisine should consider visiting such restaurants as Sakura (it specializes in Japanese cuisine), Wild Rice (Chinese food can be a masterpiece and this restaurant will prove that) or The Royal Elephant (this dining establishment is famous for its luxurious atmosphere that makes everyone feel like an oriental fairytale has come true; by the way, the restaurant specializes in Thai cuisine).

Monal Islamabad is a wonderful destination for everyone interested in authentic national food. In the opinion of many, this is the best restaurant in the city. Moreover, Monal Islamabad offers striking views of the city. If the Middle Eastern cuisine is a primary target, consider visiting Habibi. This restaurant is also one of the most attractive dining establishments in terms of price-quality. Qishmisch is one more restaurant that specializes in Pakistani and Middle Eastern cuisines. Moreover, all food is cooked in strict accordance with the Quran rules (in other words, it offers Halal food). Young people like to gather at Khiva restaurant that mostly offers Asian food. Finally,

Andaaz is another quality restaurant with delicious national cuisine and a welcoming atmosphere.

For a business meeting, it is hard to think of a better place than Zamana. At this restaurant, visitors can enjoy wonderful food and chat in a casual atmosphere that is perfect for longer talks. Romantic couples, in their turn, prefer to book a table at La Maison for a romantic dinner. The gorgeous restaurant specializes in fine French cuisine and is, without a doubt, "an oasis in Islamabad". Tourists wishing to dine at an unusual place will like Cave Dinner. This restaurant has a one-of-a-kind design it looks like a cave. That being said, this is not the only advantage of Cave Dinner as the food is simply excellent.

If local food starts to taste a bit boring and there is an urge to eat the traditional European cuisine that is not hot and spicy, The Butler restaurant is the right place to visit. This dining establishment also offers food for vegetarians. All fans of Chinese food and Chinese décor simply cannot fail to visit the restaurant with a simple name that speaks for itself Chinatown. Pappasallis is one more dining establishment that offers quality food that won't break the budget. It offers particularly delicious pizza and other Italian dishes.

In Islamabad, there is an interesting restaurant that is called Kabul. It specializes in Asian and Afghan cuisines. Many visit Kabul to eat delicious kebabs there are many varieties on the menu. The restaurant is very popular among locals. In Kabul, visitors can order interesting dishes with rice and vegetables, popular vegetable soups, and traditional bread. The dining establishment charms its guests with a pleasant and casual atmosphere that makes the restaurant perfect for vacationers with children. Among regular visitors to this restaurant, there are always many locals who come to enjoy their favorite kebab.

Islamabad Tradition and Lifestyle
Colors of Islamabad traditions, festivals, mentality and lifestyle

Residents of the capital of Pakistan are friendly and tender-hearted people. These qualities are always revealed in the way they treat tourists locals are always ready to help tourists in trouble. Of course, local people expect tourists to follow the rules of the Pakistani society. This is the right way for travelers to make everyone in Islamabad like them. Local families are united and family members are close to each other because family and friends are the main treasure for every local. They are ready to fight for their family until the end and protect their beliefs as long as they can. Leather goods, textiles, items made of wood and metal remain the traditional crafts of local people.

Tourists shouldn't have problems when dealing with locals. Almost everyone speaks English and it is hard to meet a person who cannot say even several basic phrases. Despite the fact that the capital of Pakistan is home to people of different nationalities, and some nationalities are more widespread than others, everyone is friendly to tourists. Famous Middle Eastern traditions of hospitality are not a myth here, and a refusal to come to someone's home for dinner is simply impossible. Moreover, tourists are not recommended to do that because the host will be very offended.

The capital of Pakistan regularly hosts interesting festivals that appeal not only to local people but also to tourists, many of which arrive in the city in order to visit these wonderful events. Fair trades and exhibitions are also not rare in Islamabad. They are an opportunity to make profitable deals. Shaz K & A&S Exhibition, which takes place in Ensemble apparel shop at the beginning of June, is one of the most popular events. The exhibition is dedicated to the fashion industry. Fashion shows, master classes with interesting music and dancing performances the exhibition's visitors will find all these and much more. Without a doubt, it is a wonderful opportunity for all businessmen to sign profitable contracts.

Chand Raat Mela is one of the most colorful events in Islamabad. It is held in the city in the middle of June. This is the time of never-ending fun. Chand Raat Mela is a cocktail of music, dancing, and delicious food. The festival is held at TEN 11 Lounge. For tourists, it is a unique opportunity to learn the local culture as deep as possible. Among the headliners of this event, there are many popular and famous Pakistani performers and bands, and many of them dance and sing folk songs.

Traditional Calligraphy Exhibition is one more festival that is tightly connected with the cultural heritage of the country. It usually takes place in the Heritage Museum. During the exhibition, visitors can see interesting calligraphic drawings made on leather, wood, copper, and precious metals. As a rule, the event starts at the beginning of July and ends closer to the middle of the month. Islamabad Literature Festival is also widely celebrated in the city. This event is held in Hotel Margala in the middle of April. This is the time when visitors can meet poets and novelists from Pakistan and other countries. The program features lectures, seminars, poetic evenings, readings, and art exhibitions.

A large gastronomic event takes place in the capital in the middle of April when Islamabad hosts Spring Food Festival. As a rule, this festival lasts two days and takes place in Lake-View Park. Visitors can try various local delicacies, and kids are always glad to have fun at a special playground that opens for the event. Numerous local cafes, bars, and restaurants join the event, offering their best delicacies and signature dishes. Besides an opportunity to try many interesting dishes that belong to the national cuisine, there is always a range of Indian, Chinese, and European dishes. A flower exhibition has become an essential part of the event, so all fans of flora will be delighted.

It is natural that the capital of the country hosts the largest Independence Day celebration in Pakistan. Islamabad is incredibly interesting to visit on this day. The celebration coincides with the

National Music Festival. This means that besides military parades that always take place on the central streets of the city visitors can enjoy performances of local music bands. Needless to say, this holiday is an excellent opportunity to learn more about the local culture. The music festival starts at the beginning of August while Independence Day falls to August 14. Right before the celebration, in the evening on August 13, there is always the largest music event in the schedule of the festival. This is an "opening act" of the Independence Day celebrations in Pakistan.

Shopping in Islamabad

Shopping in Islamabad authentic goods, best outlets, malls and boutiques

The largest shopping center of Islamabad is The Centaurus. Trade pavilions of the world's most famous brands are assembled there. You can purchase amazing outfits from world-famous designers, or choose beautiful Asian-style clothes at a really attractive cost. The center has many play areas for children, restaurants, and cafes with open terraces that offer a wonderful view of the mountains.

Those who don't go to overcrowded and noisy shopping centers, will appreciate Safa Gold Mall. It is distinguished by a very calm and measured environment and offers clothing and accessories of popular brands. There are jewelry and cosmetics stores, as well. The last floor of the shopping center is fully placed at the disposal of restaurants and cafes. There is an excellent supermarket on the ground floor for budget tourists.

Not far from the prestigious Kabul restaurant is a wonderful Saeed Book Bank bookstore. This three-story store offers smart booklets and books about Pakistan. Tourists can get excellent maps showing the main attractions, as well as photo albums with magnificent views and books on the history and culture of the country. The store has a fairly large department with stationery goods. You can buy bright notebooks and pens as souvenirs.

A wonderful market where you can purchase memorable gifts, is located on Garden Avenue. Here, local artists sell paintings, jewelry and costume jewelry. Women should definitely pay attention to the counters with aromatic oils and oil-based cosmetics. Still, you have a choice of wonderful local fabrics and hand-painted utensils. For the most affluent customers there are shopping pavilions with antiques.

In search of exquisite jewelry, go to Salon Libra Jewellers. This is a large and nicely decorated jewelry salon, that sell goods of local manufacturers. All of them are of quite high quality and are much cheaper than in many European countries. They present goods for every taste and purse, from miniature articles to luxurious necklaces and rings in typical Asian style, usually bought by the wealthiest visitors.

Men won't feel bored in Islamabad, as well. Outfitters store presents a large choice of men's clothing. All-year-round clothes for each season is available to customers. They sell T-shirts, shirts, coats, and jackets and have outfits not only for grown-ups but for boys of various ages. Customers receive the best value for their money.

There are many interesting art galleries in Islamabad. Because of the reduced number of traditional souvenir shops in the city, they're a real treasure for tourists who buy paintings by local artists as souvenirs. An excellent choice of paintings is presented in Tanzara Art Gallery. If you don't have money to buy a painting, you can visit the gallery just like a museum.

Until late at night, runs Aabpara market. This market is especially loved by budget tourists. Here, inexpensive clothes, including very beautiful clothes for children are sold. Women can choose inexpensive costume jewelry in a typical Pakistani style or beautiful handbags and shoes from local craftsmen. Experienced tourists advise to closely monitor the quality of the presented products. It is not always high.

There are also excellent antique shops in Islamabad. Alico Antiques is the most famous one. It will be of interest to absolutely all tourists, no matter how big a budget they have. Alongside with expensive rarities and works of art, they sell a lot of interesting old trifles at affordable prices.

Islamabad Tourist Tips

Preparing your trip to Islamabad: advices & hints things to do and to obey

1. In general, the capital of Pakistan is quite a safe city, but it is still better not to take valuables when heading to local markets and shops. Don't leave your belongings unattended because there can be thieves in public places.

2. Try to escape very crowded places. As it was mentioned above, Islamabad is a relatively safe city compared to other cities in Pakistan. However, safety should always be the number one priority.

3. As Pakistan is a Muslim country (this is even written in the country's constitution), it is better to refrain from drinking alcohol during Islamic holidays. Don't forget to follow local rules. This is particularly true about the behavior of men and women. For example, it is better if females do not walk alone without a guide or a man, especially in the evening and away from the city center. This rule doesn't apply to men, except for the second part of the recommendation. Even for men, it is better not to appear in remote areas alone in the evening.

4. Local rules regarding alcohol in public places are quite strict. It is allowed to consume alcohol only in some sports bars and in hotels. Local people disapprove even of the situations when some tourist is holding a bottle with alcohol in hands. In order not to make locals

worried, simply do not hold alcohol in a way that the bottle is visible to others. It is better to put it in a bag.

5. In order to be able to drink alcohol, even tourists need to obtain special permission. It is informally called "non-Muslim declaration". The thing is, Muslim people are prohibited to consume alcohol by the law. Christians can drink alcohol in Islamabad, but only if they have the declaration.

6. When getting acquainted with a local, let them decide if they want to shake hands or no. As a rule, local people greet each other with "Assalam Alaikum". The rule applies to both men and women. This happens because the social class of a local person is also an important factor that is taken into consideration. Don't forget that local people use only their right hand for a handshake. According to Islam, the left hand is considered impure. Stretching the left hand for a handshake might offend a local person.

7. It is very comfortable to navigate in the city using a taxi or a car (own or rented one). Taxi price goes up in the evening. This is particularly true about the Jinnah Super district. Don't forget to negotiate the price of a taxi ride with the driver in advance.

8. Such transport as metro is also very comfortable. It is easy to reach different parts of Islamabad by metro. There are Wi-Fi hotspots and a quality air conditioning system that is irreplaceable in scorching heat.

9. Vacationers can rent a car or a car with a driver. Many hotels offer this service to their clients.

10. Tips for any service are welcome, but they are not obligatory.

11. It is prohibited to take pictures or record videos of military objects, people on duty, and police stations. If you are not sure whether it is allowed to take pictures, it is better to ask locals first.

12. The most popular souvenirs and gifts that travelers prefer to bring from Islamabad are the following: salt lamps, jewelry, carpets, silk garments, ceramics, and handmade chess.

Karachi
Karachi Guide
Sightseeing in Karachi what to see. Complete travel guide
Karachi is the largest city on the Arabian coast, a famous industrial and marine port of Pakistan. Despite the arid climate that is usual for this region, the conditions here are quite comfortable. May and June are considered the hottest months. During this period the temperature of air reaches +40C. On winter the temperature rarely falls below +10C.

Main Museum is always ready to provide visitors with information about the history of the city. You will also find numerous architectural sights in Karachi. Parks of this city are home to multiple monuments, the majority of which are devoted to some notable events in the history of the city. Multiple cafes and restaurants of this city will provide you with best dishes of local chiefs. Magnificent markets are one of the main peculiarities of Karachi. This is a true paradise for all shopaholics.

Zainab Market looks like an Aladdin's cave from the famous fairytale, than like a market. Here you can find almost everything widest choice of souvenirs and crafts, wonderful pictures, Kashmir shawls, and souvenirs from onyx. Empress Bazar is considered the largest food market of the city. The freshest and most delicious fruit, vegetables, seafood and spices are sold here. Chiefs from local cafes will gladly cook the prawns and squids you've bought according to their old receipts and will also treat you with flavorings, the receipt of which is a secret. Bohri Market is full of small shops selling absolutely different stuff. Here you will find plates, jewelry, fabrics and clothes. This market is considered the largest and hardest to orient in, so when you visit it for the first time, we recommend taking a guide. So called "Combined Market" offers the largest choice of local crafts. The famous Pakistan resort offers truly wide choice of places for amazing rest.

The most popular tourist site is the peninsula of Manora. Many travelers in summer are attracted by little beaches here. On the peninsula, the area of which is only 2.5 square kilometers, there are many beautiful places for walks, and even several intriguing historical sites. The most interesting sight of these places is the Hindu temple of

Shri Varun Dev Mandir. The exact date and history of its construction are unknown. According to one of the legends, this magnificent temple was built with the funds of a rich navigator back in the 16th century. Until now, the once beautiful temple has survived partially. It is in desolation and is gradually being destroyed.

Directly on the territory of the city, there are also interesting religious sites, among which is the temple of Shri Swaminarayan Mandir. This Hindu temple is the largest in the territory of Pakistan. It covers an area of more than 32,000 square meters. This classy temple was built more than one and a half centuries ago. Everyone can visit it and appreciate its luxurious interior. Now the huge temple is a permanent place for holding important religious events.

In the vicinity of the city, there are several interesting archaeological areas, among which the most visited is Mohenjo-daro. More than 2.5 thousand years ago in this place was a large prosperous city, which was the center of the Indian civilization. In its study, archaeologists have made a lot of incredible discoveries. It turned out that for the construction of buildings in the city, the most advanced technology of those times were used. For example, the buildings here were made of burnt stone. Special technologies allowed the residents of the city to build ritual complexes of incredible proportions. Today, visitors to the archaeological area can admire the carefully restored fragments of old buildings and religious structures.

The outstanding architectural monument of the city is the Mohatta Palace. This palace was built in 1927 for one of the wealthy entrepreneurs. The palace amazes with the luxury of exterior and interior decoration. In it are preserved elegant stained-glass windows and domes, and in the walls of the palace many unique antiques and works of art are hidden. The main secret of the palace is a complex of underground tunnels.

Karachi for Family and Kids

Family trip to Karachi with children. Ideas on where to go with your child

In search of a suitable place for recreation with children in Karachi, it is worth paying attention to the entertainment center Dreamworld. It is a large modern complex on the coast with a landscaped adjoining territory. In this center, a water park is available for visitors, which has a large pool with artificial waves, as well as several indoor pavilions with attractions for children of different ages. This entertainment center is located in the territory of one of the largest hotels. It is perfectly equipped and very comfortable.

On a hot day, you can go on a vacation to the entertainment center Sindbad Amusement Park. It was one of the first centers in the city where a 3D cinema was opened. Now, in addition to the modern cinema, several gaming halls with attractions and cafes are available here for visitors. It will be difficult to find a better place than this where you can pass time in the heat of a hot day in Karachi.

For those who prefer to relax in the fresh air, it is worth going to the amusement park Chunky Monkey. This park can safely be said to be one of the most colorful and modern in the city. It is aimed specifically at visitors with young children in many ways. The choice of carousels and water slides here is simply huge. One of the attractions - catapult - is designed specifically for fans of extreme sports. Kids will have the opportunity to ride a mini-train and try out other original attractions in action.

The colorful water park Great Fiesta, in which you can comfortably relax all day, also has its attractive features. This outdoor water park is decorated with a lot of living plants. There are slender palms and exotic flowers growing everywhere. The central place in the water park is occupied by a large swimming pool, which includes several colorful water slides. While children are entertained on attractions, adults will have the opportunity to sunbathe on specially equipped terraces.

Fans of nature and animal enthusiast should definitely look into the Karachi Zoo. This zoo is located near the city center, and was opened in a picturesque garden. In this zoo, you can see tigers, lions, magnificent peacocks and waterfowl for which artificial lakes are equipped. A lot of pleasant surprises await young visitors to the zoo.

They will be able to feed miniature monkeys and even hold parrots in their hands. On the territory of the extensive garden where the zoo is located, a lot of attractions are always equipped for children.

There are many picturesque parks in the city, which are sure to please fans nature. One of the most beautiful is the Hilal Park. It attracts with its variety of landscape decorations. There are many beautiful flower beds and compositions in the park, and comfortable benches installed in the shade of trees. It will be nice to walk here with even little children. You can make a lot of beautiful photos in the park.

Another pleasant surprise - Safari Park, awaits fans of nature and outdoor recreation. In this safari park, visitors are offered an opportunity to get acquainted with typical inhabitants of the wild world. They will be able to feed elephants, see tigers that live in a spacious aviary, and feed the birds living in the lake. The safari park is located on the top of a hill, so the favorite entertainment for many of its visitors is a cable car ride. Another nice addition to the vacation will be the presence of playgrounds in the park for children.

Karachi Cultural Sights

Culture of Karachi. Places to visit old town, temples, theaters, museums and palaces

In the past, Karachi was the capital of Pakistan. As it was also a large seaport, the city was always prosperous. In Karachi, there are many ancient architectural landmarks that tourists should definitely visit. Masjid e Tooba or Tooba Mosque is one of the main symbols of the city. It is an incredibly beautiful building made of white marble that stands 70 meters above the roadway. It is not the largest mosque in Pakistan, but the building itself and adjacent terraces can provide space for more than ten thousand prayers! Some sources also claim that Masjid e Tooba is the largest single dome mosque in the world.

Karachi is also the location of one of the nation's symbols the Mausoleum of Muhammad Ali Jinnah that was built in the second half of the previous century. The complex includes a large building and a wonderful park surrounding it. The park occupies an area of more than fifty hectares. Near the mausoleum, there are tombs of the first prime minister of Pakistan Liaquat Ali Khan and Jinnah's daughter, Fatima. Numerous travelers from different regions of Pakistan come to Karachi in order to visit the last resort of the country's first president. It is quite interesting to see the change of guard at the mausoleum, explore the interesting architecture of this place, stroll in the gorgeous park, and look at the giant chandelier that is a gift from the People's Republic of China.

Even though Islam is the dominant religion in the region, there are churches and temples of other religions in Karachi, such as Holy Trinity Cathedral and the Church of St Andrew. The cathedral was built in the middle of the 19th century. For many years, the landmark was used as a lighthouse. The Church of St Andrew was built approximately at the same time. It is a wonderful example of Indian-English architecture in the Gothic style. In Karachi, there is also a sacred place of more unusual Zoroastrianism. This is the so-called Tower of Silence. In the past, bodies of dead people were left in this tower in the open air.

Saint Patrick's Cathedral is one more center of Christianity in Karachi. It is also the residence of Roman Catholic archdiocese. The church is a wonderful example of the neo-gothic style. Tourists will notice sharp turrets of the building when it is yet far away from them. Saint Patrick's Cathedral is recognized as the oldest Christian church in Pakistan. In the inner yard of the gorgeous landmark, there is a magnificent garden with fountains, summerhouse s, and benches. It is an ideal place to relax and hide from the scorching heat. Not far from the church, there is another popular landmark, Empress Market that is a wonderful place to shop souvenirs.

The Mohatta Palace is one more "must visit" tourist destination in Karachi. The fabulous building was constructed at the beginning of the 20th century. At that time, it was a summer residence of businessman Shivratan Chandraratan Mohatta. The palace is a big place its total area is roughly 2,000 square meters. Tourists can attend interesting excursions and see the elegant architecture of the landmark in detail, admire exceptional luxury of décor, enjoy a marvelous panorama of the city from the palace's balconies, and explore underground tunnels that Mohatta built to make sure that his wife could move around safely.

Karachi Municipal Corporation Building is one of the most famous architectural landmarks in Karachi. An interesting fact it took more than 30 years to build it. The building works started in 1895, and the official opening of the Municipal Corporation Building took place only on January 7, 1932. The fabulous design of the building is one of its major eye-catching details. Made in Baroque style, the building has grandiose cupolas, a tall tower with a clock, Doric columns, and an elegant terrace at the west wing. When it is getting dark, fabulous illumination makes the building even more attractive.

As Karachi is an important seaport, its history is full of numerous events that had a great impact on the development of the country. Pakistan Maritime Museum will tell you the interesting history of the city and the country in general. The complex consists of several galleries and halls that occupy an area of 30 hectares. The exhibition includes traditional items, such as sculptures, bas-reliefs, and images, and has a collection dedicated to modern technologies, such as new onboard digital computers. At the museum, visitors can also see Pakistan Navy's Minesweeper ship, PNS Hangor submarine, and Breguet Atlantic airplane.

Karachi Attractions and Nightlife

City break in Karachi. Active leisure ideas for Karachi attractions, recreation and nightlife

As a rule, travelers visit Karachi not only to get acquainted with local culture and attend natural and manmade landmarks but also to relax and swim in the sea. Sandspit is one of the most popular beaches in the region. It is a truly paradise-like place. The beach has gorgeous underwater life, so it is always incredibly exciting to try scuba diving in the reefs. In the first winter month, the coast area becomes a giant nesting spot of big sea turtles, so it is important to be very careful when walking on sand. The coastline that is very comfortable for relaxation, clean water, and fine sand make this beach very attractive for vacationers.

Paradise Point Beach is located in the bay with the same name. This beach is located within the city boundaries. The sea is calm here, and so the water is almost always still. However, the storm season starts in May, and this calm beach becomes the gathering place of surfers who come to ride waves. If you are fond of surfing and want to try it, it is hard to think of a better time and place. There are also areas for playing volleyball and basketball, a diving club, a horse and camel riding area, and numerous cafes and restaurants. Visitors are usually pleased with clean water and sand. However, Paradise Point Beach is popular, so if you don't like crowded places it is better to visit it early in the morning or in the evening.

Empress Market is located not far from the Saint Andrew Church in Karachi. It is a large complex that includes numerous rows of shopping stalls and one roofed pavilion. Without a doubt, this is the noisiest place in the city. Moreover, it is possible to find virtually everything here: souvenirs, clothing, and fresh fruit and vegetables. The market was opened in this building yet at the end of the 19th century. Empress Market got its name after Victoria, Queen of the United Kingdom and Empress of India. When heading to the market, don't forget about safety measures.

The local zoo is open almost in the heart of Karachi. It is one of the largest zoos in the region. Visitors can see animals from different countries and regions, including rare species from the Red List. Spacious cages have comfortable conditions that are close to the natural habitat of animals, so they can survive in the hot local climate. In the zoo, there is a wonderful park with benches, several cafes, recreation areas, and playgrounds for children. It is even allowed to pet and feed some animals.

Port Grand Food and Entertainment Complex is one of the most popular recreation and entertainment complexes in Karachi. Visitors can try various attractions, participate in competitions, dine in restaurants and cafes, visit numerous shops, and then head to a party in a nightclub. An interesting fact: the complex is open in the territory of Napier Mole, the bridge built at the beginning of the 19th century that is an important architectural landmark. There are numerous minibars where visitors can freely buy and try more than a hundred variations of alcoholic drinks (only visitors aged 21 and older are eligible).

The Chaukhandi tombs are a unique complex of great archaeological and historic value. These are tombs of the ancient tribe of Jokhio. The area was used as a burial site between the 15th and 18th centuries. The style of buildings is unique it can be found only in the province of Sindh and nowhere else in the world. Skillful stone carving that depicts scenes of battles and hunting, as well as elegant ornaments, are among the most notable symbols of this place. You can order an excursion to the tombs and admire not only ancient buildings but also picturesque landscapes.

Manora Peninsula, which is located close to Karachi, is a wonderful place with clean beaches and picturesque nature. The coastal area doesn't have a developed tourist infrastructure at the moment as it is yet under development, but it is incredibly pleasant to relax on wild beaches. It would also be a mistake not to mention a relict mangle forest located on the west side of the peninsula, the municipality of Clifton and Kiamari Town on the east side. Finally, many travelers will be excited to visit Salehabad, a small fishing village where visitors can fish. If you ask locals for directions, you can also reach Shri Varun Dev Mandir, a gorgeous Hindu temple.

Karachi Cuisine and Restaurant

Cuisine of Karachi for gourmets. Places for dinner best restaurants

The national cuisine of Pakistan combines peculiarities of Arabian and Indian cuisines, so pastries, dried fruit, and meat dishes with various spices are the core dishes in the region. Karachi is one of the biggest megalopolises in the world with a population of roughly 20 million people. Because of that, fast food chains are very widespread in the city, but there are many smaller restaurants with authentic cuisine. Moreover, there are smaller open-air cafes that cook food in front of passersby on small and silent pedestrian streets of the city. As a rule, these cafes usually offer fresh flatbread and kebab.

It is important to mention that you will hardly find pork meat in most regions of Pakistan. This limitation is connected to the fact that there are many Muslim people in the country. However, many tourists may not even notice that because local dining establishments use various types of meat, such as beef, chicken, mutton, and goat. Flatbread with meat, vegetables, and spicy sauce is the most popular quick meal in the city and a typical local "fast food". When it comes to spices, curry and different types of pepper, especially chili pepper, are the most popular here. Vegetables are a typical garnish in the country, but local chefs can also use beans and grits.

Without a doubt, Biryani is a very interesting and unusual dish that travelers can try in Karachi. It is a second-course dish that is similar to pilaf at a glance. It also contains rice, meat, and vegetables. However, Biryani also contains yogurt that adds a special soft and creamy taste. By the way, the dish can taste differently in different restaurants in the city. This happens because of different spices used every Pakistani cook has their own signature set of spices mixed in different proportions. Because of this peculiarity, it is hard to find dishes that taste identically. Even if the recipe is the same, each dish will have its unique aroma and taste.

It would be a mistake not to mention a variety of flatbreads that are available virtually everywhere in Karachi. Flatbreads can be cooked in a number of ways; they can contain different flour, sauces, spices, and garnish. A pleasant aroma of freshly made flatbreads is often noticeable in the city, attracting numerous buyers. You can try local bread as a separate dish and together with other products. Either way, you will not be disappointed by the unusual taste of traditional Pakistani flatbreads.

Currently, there are limitations regarding alcohol in Pakistan. It is possible to buy it in special shops only. That being said, tourists can try many other interesting and original drinks in Karachi. For example, there are many tea houses in the city because locals are fans of this hot and fragrant drink. Serving methods can be different in different tea houses. Tea can contain spices, herbs, fruit, milk, and a lot of sugar. Lassi is an unusual drink that is also widespread in the region. It contains yogurt, minced vegetables, sugar, and salt. Lassi is particularly popular in summer because it is exceptionally good in quenching thirst.

Just like in many other Islamic countries, sweet tooths will be super excited here as the variety of national sweets is simply astonishing. Most of them have an unusual and pleasant taste that is very addictive. Barfi is a very popular dessert in the region. It contains milk and various fillings. Tourists should also try Mitai candies containing flour, syrups, and cream; Raita a universal dish with cream that can be consumed even together with second-course dishes, and various sorbets, pies, and sponge cakes. Vacationers should keep in mind that local Halva is a dessert containing carrots, eggs, nuts, and cream.

Kolachi Restaurant is one of the most popular dining establishments in the city. It is an authentic restaurant that offers a range of Pakistani, Afghani, Asian, and Middle Eastern cuisines. It is the right place for everyone who wants to eat fresh seafood and juicy kebabs. Moreover, the restaurant is located in a picturesque place that offers a fantastic view of the coast. The menu is diverse and contains options for different groups of guests. There are suitable dishes for vegans, vegetarians, gluten-free food, and Halal dishes suitable for Muslims.

BBQ Tonight is a popular café that is equally suitable for breakfast, lunch, and dinner. Open in a peaceful part of the city, this café is perfectly suitable for meetings with friends and business partners. It is a perfectly suitable place to try many dishes of traditional Pakistani and Afghani cuisines, see how skillful cooks make barbecue or try meat cooked over an open fire. The charming design of this café is perfect for relaxing and enjoying a pleasant meal. The menu contains dishes for vegetarians, Halal food, and gluten-free food.

Karachi Tradition and Lifestyle

Colors of Karachi traditions, festivals, mentality and lifestyle

Karachi is a city with a very interesting history that is full of events. It was the capital of independent Pakistan and lost this title only in the second half of the previous century. However, Karachi hasn't lost its importance even nowadays. Currently, it is the center of an important administrative region. As many spheres of life are well-developed in Karachi, numerous people from smaller towns want to move to it, find a job in Karachi, and settle here. The process of urbanization is very active in the country, and large cities develop and grow fast. Karachi is no exception it is one of the biggest cities in the world at the moment and the seventh biggest urban agglomeration.

If you were expecting to find a calm and steady city, you will be disappointed because active life and hectic atmosphere are typical in modern Karachi. It is safe to say that this city never sleeps. You will be surprised to see how active local people are. They will always be in a hurry, try to sell something to you, walk fast, or do something else. Despite the fact that several dozen different nations with different traditions and religions live in Pakistan, local people are quite peaceful and are, in general, quite tolerant of foreigners.

The majority of people in the country are Muslims, and this fact shapes the everyday life of the region because this religion implies strict following the rules stipulated in the sacred books. For example, it is very hard to find dishes with pork in Pakistan because this animal is considered impure in Islamic culture. It is not rare to see people praying right on the streets. Other people may spontaneously join the prayer, and this applies not only to passersby but also to drivers of public transport. The Pakistanis are very religious people, and so it is very important for them to follow the traditions of Islam.

Local people treat tourists with respect and interest. They are ready to forgive small mistakes in local etiquette and rules if tourists make them unintentionally. However, vacationers shouldn't speak vile of local traditions and culture. The same applies to criticizing the religion they will definitely express their disapproval. In Karachi, tourists will have no problems with communication if they can speak basic English, just like in many big cities around the world. However, English might be useless in the countryside even though many signs have copies in other languages. According to statistics, only one-fifth of Pakistan's population knows English.

It is important to follow some simple rules that are typical for any Muslim country: do not touch other people without any particular purpose, do not take items with the left hand, do not walk in front of praying people, do not point at other people with shoe soles, and do not enter the female part of the house if someone invites you to visit their house. It is also better to learn more about gestures that have a negative meaning in the region. Some gestures that are innocent for European and American countries may be regarded as offensive in Pakistan.

There are no limitations regarding the clothing, but it is still not recommended to wear too revealing and extravagant outfits. This is particularly true about women. When visiting a mosque, all parts of the body except feet must be covered. Women also need to put a scarf on their head. Smoking is banned in virtually all public areas. If you need to smoke, search for permitting signs first. Vacationers should also not forget that toilet paper is not used in Pakistan. Instead of it, there are bidets or simply water containers (because this is approved by the Quran). Bathtubs are also virtually nonexistent because locals use shower cabins.

Every year, Karachi hosts a literature festival that is held at Beach Luxury Hotel. The popular event lasts two days in the first week of

February. During the festival, all participants can discuss various books, watch presentations of new bestsellers, and meet authors who promote their latest works. Vacationers can also participate in master classes and discussions, watch musical and theatrical performances dedicated to famous books, or simply enjoy reading. The event is quite popular, so it is not rare to see guests from other countries at the festival.

Every year, the area in front of the Karachi Metropolitan Corporation Building becomes the location of Hamara Karachi. It is a popular festival with its own interesting program of events. As a rule, it includes a small parade, some thematic exhibition, sampling local delicacies, concerts, and other festivities. The first celebration Hamara Karachi was so grandiose that even the president of the country visited it.

Shopping in Karachi
Shopping in Karachi authentic goods, best outlets, malls and boutiques
Dolmen Mall Clifton is the most popular shopping center in Karachi. It has an eye-catching design and offers a range of goods for any taste and budget. There are attractive shops with European style clothing and shopping pavilions that sell elegant clothing in the national style. Men will like Gordano, a popular store that offers a range of quality clothing in the national style. There is also a large Mango shop in

Dolmen Mall. The shopping complex regularly organizes interesting events for visitors. There are nice cafes, as well as numerous playgrounds and attractions for children.

Port Grand Shopping and Entertainment complex can compete for the honorable title of the most prestigious shopping center in Karachi. The complex has an eye-catching and original design. Port Grand is the location of prestigious designer boutiques that supply fashionistas with new exclusive outfits. There are also high-quality restaurants that have their tables inside and outside in the open air, in a picturesque adjacent territory. Budget tourists will also find it interesting to visit this shopping center because there are interesting souvenir shops and attractions for children. Outside, there are food carts with inexpensive street food.

Many tourists and locals head to Atrium Mall to shop and have fun. This mall has a selection of inexpensive clothing and shoe stores that offer quality items. Women will be excited to visit jewelry shops and stores with inexpensive fashion jewelry. Atrium Malls also has a food court and one of the most popular cinemas in Karachi.

Tourists who prefer to shop in calm and non-crowded places will definitely like Dolmen Mall Tariq Road. This shopping complex is located at a distance from vibrant central streets of the city, so locals are the main visitors in Dolmen Mall Tariq Road. There are interesting and modern shops that offer clothing and accessories in European style, as well as shops with traditional clothes and accessories in the national style. Consider visiting a large electronics store and an inexpensive supermarket on the ground floor of the building. The latter is great for budget tourists.

Karachi is famous for its colorful markets, and Zainab Market is one of the largest in the city. There are rows of shopping stalls with clothing, bags, and accessories that are available at some of the lowest prices in the city. Many travelers visit this market in order to shop for jewelry created by local artisans the jewelry is really attractive but it doesn't cost much. This is one of the oldest markets in Karachi, so there are many stalls with popular local delicacies and various spices.

There are many interesting souvenir shops in the city, and Tali Karachi is definitely one of them. In this shop, visitors will find unique artworks created by the best artisans in the city. Tourists may be interested in manually embroidered colorful pillows, interesting clay artworks, painted plates, beautiful paintings, wooden home décor items, and many other interesting accessories in the national style.

If the book is the best memorable gift from a vacation in Karachi for you, then you may find it very exciting to visit Tit Bit Book Stall. This is a popular bookstore that offers many interesting books on different subjects. As a rule, tourists enjoy buying books and albums dedicated to the history and culture of Pakistan. The opening of this shop took place yet in the 40s of the previous century. Since that time, Tit Bit

Book Stall has become a true landmark of the city. This bookstore has always been owned by the same family. It offers not only popular books but also modern magazines, and colorful comic books.

When describing local markets, it would be a mistake not to mention Paradise Market that is perfectly suitable for travelers in search of unusual souvenirs. At this market, travelers can find interesting antique items, inexpensive vintage tableware, jewelry, artworks, and other antiquities. Even experienced antiquity collectors will find it interesting to visit this market

Karachi Tourist Tips
Preparing your trip to Karachi: advices & hints things to do and to obey

1. Pakistan is considered quite a dangerous country for tourists, and an unstable political climate only adds to this situation. Karachi is one of the potentially unsafe regions, so if you want to visit this city it is important to observe safety measures strictly.

2. Always have an identity document and a visa with you. In Pakistan, there are quite many patrols that can ask you to show your documents. Travelers do not need to be scared of them these patrols are quite loyal to tourists.

3. It is better to keep a distance from crowds of people, all kinds of strikes and meetings. Otherwise, you may be mistaken for a member

of some radical group. It is also a good idea to stay away from the buildings of local authorities and objects controlled by the army.

4. Don't forget about safety measures during your vacation in the country: do not take big sums of money when going outside, do not show off your expensive items and walk on the city's streets at night. Besides that, it is better to exchange currency only in special exchange offices, such as banks, hotels, and official exchange points. Do not use exchange services of individuals because there is a risk of getting scammed.

5. When planning an excursion outside the city, it is better to hire a guide. When searching for a guide, don't forget to check the presence of a license that is mandatory in the country. As a last resort, it is possible to find a guide at local tour agencies.

6. It is strongly not recommended to take pictures of military objects, police and army forces, inner décor of mosques, important strategic objects (such as bridges, airports), and Pakistani women. It is possible to take pictures of local people only if they give you permission.

7. Sometimes tourists must have a special permit to be able to explore some mountain regions and valleys. That being said, access to some regions is prohibited for all travelers. It is important to think of a route carefully and find out about restricted areas in advance. The period

starting from May until October is considered the best time to visit the mountains.

8. As a rule, tips are already included in the total in Karachi, and 10% is a typical service fee in the country. However, tourists can leave some extra (around 5%) at local restaurants and cafes if they want to thank the friendly staff. A typical tip for taxi drivers is 10% (it is better to specify the price of a ride in advance). Porters will be glad to receive 10 rupees for their services. However, if you plan to leave the city and visit the countryside, it may be better not to give tips at all because they may be considered as an offense.

9. Tourists should apply for a Pakistan visa beforehand and only in their country of residence. Pakistan embassies abroad are likely to reject applications. You will also need an invitation from Pakistan. Most tour agencies offer this service.

10. When filling the visa application form, don't forget to mention all the cities in Pakistan that you plan to visit. Tourists can visit Karachi, Multan, Islamabad, Lahore, and their neighborhoods. Such destinations as Tribal Area, Balochistan, and territories close to the borders have limitations for tourists.

11. Karachi has a well-developed system of public buses. It is easy to reach any part of the city by public transport. There are also stations for intercity rides that sell tickets to other settlements of the country.

12. Blackouts are not rare in many cities in Pakistan, including big ones. Karachi is no exception, so it is a good idea to take a couple of spare batteries and power banks.

The End

Printed in the USA
CPSIA information can be obtained
at www.ICGtesting.com
LVHW040235060224
771075LV00024B/215